God's Grace for Every Family is th   k
needed for every single parent long   h
church body coming alongside. A   in
a way no other book on this topic has addressed, while also finding
practical, biblical help for the struggles and burdens of single parenting.
Weaving together story, Scripture, and research, Anna Meade Harris
answers the question every church and lay leader should ask: How can
we embrace and love single parents in our community? *God's Grace for
Every Family* will be a powerful resource for many!

> **Lisa Appelo,** single mom to seven and author of *Life Can
> Be Good Again: Putting Your World Back Together After It
> All Falls Apart*

No two single parents share the same circumstances. But they share
many of the same needs from their brothers and sisters in Christ in the
church. Anna Meade Harris offers gospel-centered perspective that will
not only encourage her fellow single parents but also equip the rest of us
to love them well. This book is full of godly counsel and hard-earned,
practical wisdom.

> **Collin Hansen,** vice president of content and editor in chief of
> The Gospel Coalition, author of *Timothy Keller: His Spiritual
> and Intellectual Formation,* host of the *Gospelbound* podcast

I don't know of a church without single-parent families, and yet I know
of very few resources on how churches can minister to those families.
In this book, Anna Meade Harris doesn't treat single-parent families
as a math problem—a mere subtraction of one parent. With biblical
knowledge and personal experience, she shows us the unique ministry
needs single-parent families have. And she gives us solutions and ideas.
This is a welcome book for Christians who want to welcome the single-
parent families they love.

> **Russell Moore,** *Christianity Today*

This book takes me back . . . back to my parents' divorce when I was
fifteen, and then the subsequent years of living with my now-single
mom. The Scriptures and stories are honest and unfiltered. Without
superficiality or pat answers, Anna continually points us to the hope,
strength, and healing that only God can provide.

> **Dr. Rob Rienow,** founder of Visionary Family Ministries

Many tears welled up reading this unique, important book on an under-served theme. Tears of pain for the journey single families walk. Tears of lament for the way leaders like me have been complicit in the loneliness and isolation. Tears of hope because of the stories of light beyond the loss. Tears of thankfulness because, as Anna testifies, the enough-ness of Jesus really is enough. This book is equal parts storytelling and Bible study, everywhere soaked through with the gospel. Every pastor . . . no, every Christian, needs to read it.

> **Zac Hicks,** pastor of Church of the Cross
> (Birmingham, Alabama) and author of several books,
> including *Before We Gather*

Beginning *God's Grace for Every Family*, I immediately identified those who would benefit from reading it: my recently divorced neighbor, my recently widowed friend. When I finished this book, however, I'd gained a much deeper appreciation for the gospel and the comfort it offers to all kinds of readers. Through stories of single parents, Harris helps us trust God's plentiful provision and presence in seasons of need. Moreover, she inspires and instructs the church to act as God's hands and feet. Biblically faithful, intensely practical, and personally vulnerable, *God's Grace for Every Family* is a book I heartily recommend.

> **Jen Pollock Michel,** author of *A Habit Called Faith*
> and *In Good Time*

Anna Harris has written the definitive book for single parents. In a corpus of literature that tells weary single parents to pick themselves up by their bootstraps, Anna points them to the Lord Christ, who carries their load. This book is a well of hope, relief, and mercy, all grounded in Scripture. No better Christian book for single parents has ever been written.

> **Cameron Cole,** chairman of Rooted Ministries

GOD'S GRACE

FOR EVERY FAMILY

GOD'S GRACE

FOR EVERY FAMILY

Biblical Encouragement for Single-Parent Families
and the Churches That Seek to Love Them Well

ANNA MEADE HARRIS

To Mac, Sam, and Ben:

Love will hold us together,
make us a shelter to weather the storm,
And I'll be my brother's keeper,
so the whole world will know that we're not alone.
—MATT MAHER AND STEVE WILSON

*To the many friends who have cared for
us and continue to care for us:
We share our story in the hope that other families
will be loved as well as we have been.
You know who you are. We love you too.*

*And in honor of all the single moms and dads
out there who want nothing more than to lead
their children to Jesus and love them well:*

"May those who love you be secure.
May there be peace within your walls
and security within your citadels."
For the sake of my family and friends,
I will say, "Peace be within you."
—PSALM 122:6–8

Contents

Introduction

My Family's Story

The LORD has done great things for us,
and we are filled with joy. . . .
Those who sow with tears
will reap with songs of joy.
Those who go out weeping,
carrying seed to sow,
will return with songs of joy,
carrying sheaves with them. (Psalm 126:3, 5–6)

In December 2010, my husband, Jeff, died after a fourteen-month battle with colon cancer. Our boys were nine, twelve, and thirteen years old.

It has been thirteen years since my boys watched a football game or played Rook with their dad. He did not teach them to drive a car. He never met their college roommates. He did not pray with them before debate or sports tournaments, nor did he take them to see any of the new Star Wars movies.

As for me, thirteen years is a long time to be without the other person who loves your kids as much as you do.

One day, when Jeff's suffering was intense, I made the senseless comment that I wished I were the one who was sick instead of him. Hugging me close, he said, "I wish we could trade places too. Where I am going will be so much better than being here.

You'll be left behind and carry on alone. I have a wonderful future ahead. Yours is going to be a lot harder."

On the one hand, his words encouraged me. Jeff believed death would take him straight into the presence of Jesus, whom he trusted for his salvation and eternal security. For a man who wanted to stay with his family as much as he did to understand that being with Jesus would be even better, well, that was a testimony.

I also heard his love for me, that he would give me the better part, being with Jesus, if he could.

But Jeff spoke from experience. His own parents divorced when he was twelve. Jeff knew the pain of not having both parents at home. Along with his brother and sister, he struggled through difficult seasons when his mom and dad did not live in the same town. Living with his mom, Jeff loved her but also worried about her, in the way of sons who feel extra responsibility in a dad's absence. The last thing Jeff wanted was for his own boys to grow up fatherless or for his wife to raise them husbandless.

As a child, Jeff had lived the struggles I would encounter as a single parent. Our particular story looked different from his; certainly divorce, death, abandonment, adoption, or any other event that leads to parenting alone will bring with it particular nuances for each family. Over the years, as I met other single moms and dads, I became curious about their stories and struggles. I learned that our families have much in common. Single parents want nothing more than to love their children, to provide and protect, to see them heal and thrive, but doing that alone seems virtually impossible. At times, that impossibility threatens to break our hearts.

This book grew out of those conversations. After losing Jeff, I was a desperate, overwhelmed wreck of a mom. One day at a time, the steadfast love of our Father God caught me, held me, and set me on my feet again. I found God's Word to be personally and in-the-moment true for my family in our everyday life of carpools and homework and grief. His promises, which once seemed frustratingly abstract, became our reality. God met our weakness with his strength, and we found that his grace is enough.

In these pages I celebrate what my boys and I learned about the steadfast love of God for single parents and their children and invite the rest of the church to witness his grace made visible in our families.

But before I could appreciate God's grace for myself, I had to discover how limited and needy I truly am.

Facing My Not-Enoughness

In the surreal moments right after Jeff died, my boys and I made our way to the big couch in the den, where we always piled together to snuggle as a family. The youngest took his place in my lap, but there was only one lap. Two arms, three boys, and no way to hold them all as closely as I wanted to. It was the awful first of many moments when I confronted the reality that, by myself, I was not enough.

We settled in silence, disoriented by the absence of Jeff's weight and warmth amid our tangled arms and legs. Then my middle son—always the first to call it like he sees it—said quietly, "Well, I guess this means we're not a family anymore."

My brokenhearted boys thought they had lost their father and their family in one night.

I explained to them that their dad was still their dad, only he was in heaven, talking face-to-face with Jesus about us now. While we would look different without Dad around, we were still a family who belonged to each other.

Before Jeff died, we held a particular perspective of family, defined by what we saw in church and community: a mom, a dad, and at least one kid. My son was right. We didn't fit that mold anymore. It took years for us to feel reestablished as a family, even longer for that family to be more about the people present than the person absent. As I struggled to help my sons feel secure, I was always aware of all that I could not be for them.

I was not enough because I was not a man. Don't boys need a man to show them how to be men?

I was not enough because I was not a father. I was not enough because I was not *their* father.

I was not enough because kids are supposed to have two parents, and I couldn't be anything other than my finite, singular self. Four loving arms had become only two, and my reach felt so limited and weak.

Time, money, wisdom, energy, patience, you name it—the single parent constantly confronts and grieves their inability to give or to be enough.

Fear

When C. S. Lewis's wife died, he wrote, "No one ever told me that grief felt so like fear. I am not afraid, but the sensation is like being afraid."[1] With all apologies to Lewis, my grief felt like fear because I *was* afraid.

After Jeff died, I started keeping a journal. Writing out my prayers helped me concentrate when my mind felt foggy and my life surreal. Reading through that journal now, I see that worry and fear dominated my thoughts. I begged God for reassurance that my children's lives were not ruined forever, that I would not fail them when they needed me most. I had never been so afraid in my life.

How will I support our family? What if we don't have enough?

How can I meet my sons' needs? What *are* their needs? Which kid needs me most today?

Why do they fight so much? Why do they fight *me* so much? What if they grow up hating each other? Hating me? Will it always be this awful? This lonely? Who will help me? How am I going to help my kids grow up? Is there any hope for us? Are my boys' lives ruined? Will we ever be happy again?

All parents experience some degree of fear for their children. The single parent must fight fear with the truth of the gospel all day every day, alone.

Grief

Initially I thought our shared grief would bring the boys and me together. I envisioned returning often to that big couch in the den, snuggling up to talk about how much we missed Dad. That pretty much never happened. We were four different people missing Jeff four different ways. All the stages you read about—anger, denial, isolation, bargaining, and depression—they're all real, only they aren't parts of a checklist you can mark off as the term *stage* implies. The early days of grief felt like we were four balls pinging helplessly around inside a pinball machine, hitting the stages at random, only there were no bells or lights, and you only wanted your turn to be over.

Each of us had a default stage, the grief mode where we camped out more than any other. One son went in his room and stayed there, only coming out occasionally to tell us he was fine, everything was fine. Another seemed perpetually furious, slamming doors and throwing things and unable to sleep. My sons were by turns withdrawn, enraged, wistful, and sad, or sometimes just their usual selves.

The awfulness was exhausting. It seemed our different ways of coping were driving us further and further away from each other. I worried for a long time that grief would destroy the family I was trying so hard to preserve.

No matter how a mom or dad comes to parent alone, grief affects every member of the family at some point. If they hope to find comfort in Christ, single parents must learn how to lament to God and teach their children that he hears their cries.

Exhaustion

At times I longed to run and hide somewhere (literally, like in my bed—or, better yet, a bed in a hotel somewhere out of state) until some adult showed up to help me. But I knew that no backup was coming. Every single household chore, from flat tires to taxes to the broken garbage disposal, was mine to handle. Every tornado siren, freak snowstorm, trip to the ER, and call from the school was my emergency to respond to. I was on call 24/7/365. I wanted to care for my children, but bearing total responsibility felt overwhelming. The sheer physical demands of being my sons' only parent wore me out, but the mental and emotional toll was even higher. Worrying about my kids into the wee hours of the morning drained me daily. Just when they needed more from me, I had much less to give and no one to share the responsibilities with.

Single parents are dog-tired pretty much all the time.

Loneliness

Just as busyness and grief drove the boys and me apart, our new life seemed to distance us from friends in two-parent families. Living in a family without a father and husband made us feel odd, even among those closest to us. To make matters worse, suddenly

I was far busier than other moms I knew. I couldn't even relax on Saturday afternoons: I would watch two innings of one son's game, then run to another field to catch two more innings of another son's game, then leave to pick up my third son at a birthday party. One of the greatest days of my single-mom life was when my two baseball players finally played on the same team because it meant I could slow down, watch two sons in the same game, and catch up with friends on the bleachers.

Being out in the world felt lonely; being home was lonely too. My husband had traveled frequently for work and kept long hours at the office. I managed our household on my own, but I always knew he was coming home.

And now he never would again.

Weekdays were manageable. Sunlight and schedules kept us moving forward, however numb we might feel. Nights were a different story. Most nights I carried the weight of unsolved problems up the stairs with me to bed, alone. I woke up alone, with all the unshared, unresolved worries still festering in my brain.

Weekends were the absolute, hands-down worst because weekends are family time. All the wide-open free time of Saturday and Sunday became space to fill with a fun (inexpensive) family activity no one but me had interest in doing. Weekend nights are often couple time, but I was no longer part of a couple. Trying to pick a movie that satisfied all three boys was impossible. They agreed on ordering pizza but not the place we should order it from. (At least they all wanted meat-lovers pie. Thank God for bacon.)

Friday and Monday swapped places, with Friday being the day to dread and Monday being the return to at least some routine that I didn't have to plan. The only thing worse than weekends was summertime, which was basically an endless Friday afternoon. I remember looking at the front door in the evenings, gripped with an irrational yearning for Jeff to walk through it. My person was gone. He was never coming back.

Even with all that, the hurdle of Sunday morning at church felt downright unfair.

Sunday mornings were some of the hardest of the week. Church no longer felt like a refuge. All the other families in the pews had a mom and a dad, reminding us of what we had lost. Everyone was warm and kind, but in the one place we most needed to belong, we no longer fit in.

God's original design called for families to have a mom and a dad. When that's not your reality, it hurts. Our pride, envy, and self-pity threaten to separate single-parent families from the community we desperately need, but to make matters worse, that community doesn't know quite what to make of us anymore.

For me, the longest-lasting, hardest challenge of all was, and is, the loneliness.

Vulnerability

A couple of weeks after Jeff died, I made plans to walk with a friend who had been widowed two years earlier. She was raising three girls on her own, all at similar ages to my boys.

As we hit the trail near her house, her first words brought clarity to a feeling I had but could not yet name: "Anna, do you realize how *vulnerable* we are?"

Boy, did I ever. A big part of my overwhelming weariness came from constant vigilance against threats, both real and imagined, to my family's safety and well-being.

My husband had strengths that I don't have. He was an astute financial planner for our family. An attorney by trade, he was assertive and forthright. When we had choices to make for our kids, he brought his own deep love for our kids, his wisdom, and his experience to the discussion. We disagreed plenty of times, and our differences caused problems we had to work through.

But by and large we stood together, like the four legs of a table, supporting our sons and giving them stability. Now our family "table" was hopelessly off balance, and I had to be careful about any outside support I invited in to help stabilize our family. Protecting my kids was one of my highest priorities, and yet caring well for them meant I sometimes had to rely on other adults for help. Praying for discernment, I turned to other Christians for their wisdom and counsel.

Single moms and dads feel more exposed to the "slings and arrows of outrageous fortune" than married parents do. Statistically speaking, our children are more vulnerable to certain struggles than their peers from married-parent homes. (We'll cover that in the next chapter.) It's no wonder some single parents fall prey to hyper-protectiveness, while others feel defeated by the fight to keep their kids safe.

Uncertainty

Before Jeff got sick I thought of myself as a decisive person, one who could pull herself up by her bootstraps and do hard things. Even as a married woman I was pretty independent. I paid the bills, I did the chores, I made decisions. I handled things.

Or so I thought. Jeff's illness and death flattened me. Assuming total responsibility for our children, our home, our finances—everything—was overwhelming. I did not have a sounding board, or backup, or someone to push back on my decisions—except my kids, who suddenly argued with me all the time. Was this just puberty? Anger over losing their dad? I had no clue.

Self-doubt paralyzed me, and I poured out my uncertainty onto the pages of my journal. I wanted God to sit down at the kitchen table with me and tell me what to do. (I am still waiting on the answer to that prayer.) I wanted to be strong and self-assured for my children; instead, I second-guessed myself at every turn. After being blindsided by their father's cancer diagnosis, my boys needed me to be steady and reliable. Instead, I felt weak, indecisive, and worn out.

Single parents crave wisdom, ever mindful that while they bear total responsibility for their decisions, their children will share the consequences. Those who co-parent sometimes have the added burden of making decisions that go against those of their child's other parent, and then enforcing their decisions against resistance.

Shame

When I was a married parent, I rarely had to ask for outside help. My husband and I mostly took care of what our family needed, and we could afford a babysitter when we wanted extra support. At worst, I would trade support with other moms: I'll watch your kids this morning if you watch mine this afternoon.

As a single parent, I was always short of what I needed to care for my children in the way I wanted to, and that felt like failure. I was ashamed of my inadequacy at every turn. I could ask for help, but I probably couldn't return the favor. I felt like I was constantly letting my kids down. My first parents' night at the junior high was brutal: as I literally ran through two different schedules for two different kids, I hardly managed to meet any of their teachers. The next day I heard the boys' disappointment after school: "Mom, my math teacher said she didn't even see you there." That was bad: my kids needed to be on good terms with their math teachers because I was incapable of helping with math homework. That would have been their father's job. No matter what I did, I was never enough.

My weakness as a disciplinarian also caused me no end of

shame. A people pleaser by nature, I never did a good job of laying down the law and enforcing it. I felt powerless to compel the boys' obedience and feared the trouble they would get into if I didn't tame my teenage boys. The worst was the shame I felt because my sons knew how weak I was. By God's grace, they did not take advantage of me, but they could have.

Jesus is not ashamed to call us brothers and sisters, but it's hard to avoid shame when our sins, missteps, and limitations cause our children pain (Heb. 2:11).

Pride

Asking for help stinks. I know Christians aren't supposed to think that way, but I wanted to be enough for my kids all by myself. It seemed I constantly relied on the kindness of others. Even worse, there was no way I could "pay back" all the favors and the support that friends gave me. I baked chocolate chip cookies by the dozens as thank-yous when I felt I had been too needy or asked for too many rides home for my kids. I hated feeling that I owed debts I couldn't pay. It was one thing to let Jesus pay the debt for my sins—that was surely a debt beyond any means I had. But all the carpooling, changing of out-of-reach lightbulbs, heavy lifting around the house—these little kindnesses embarrassed me, and my good cookies were my only hope to even the score.

Additionally, I did not want my kids to struggle in any public way because I thought that meant I wasn't doing a very good job as their mother. After all, if they got in trouble, as their sole parent, I clearly did not have the respect and obedience of my children. It sounds silly now, but I took their behavior and thriving as my report card on how well I was leading them through this terrible time in our lives. On good days I was earning maybe a C-minus.

Married parents and single people struggle with pride too.

But the pride of a single parent takes the added toll of burdening everyone in the family to perform well so that no one can pity their weakness.

God Sets the Lonely in His Family

The first years after Jeff died were brutal. It's hard to describe how desperate I felt for our family. I despaired that we would destroy each other in our grief and loneliness. I worried that my children would turn their backs on the God who let this happen. At times I was certain they would turn their backs on each other. It seemed impossible that God would restore us to himself or to each other. For us as individuals, and for us as a family, it seemed we couldn't expect or even hope for joy to return.

But—spoiler alert—the words of Psalm 126 hang over this chapter:

> The LORD has done great things for us,
>   and we are filled with joy. . . .
> Those who sow with tears
>   will reap with songs of joy.
> Those who go out weeping,
>   carrying seed to sow,
> will return with songs of joy,
>   carrying sheaves with them. (vv. 3, 5–6)

But the Lord has done great things for us, and we are filled with joy. In our need, he has given us himself, and he has given us his church.

As the answer to my not-enoughness, God our Father has been more than enough. When I go to him, in prayer or in his Word, he meets me there. In the songs we sing at church, in our neighborhood Bible study, in texts from faithful friends, he gives me what I need when I need it. He is present in the dark of night, and in a screaming match with an angry teenager, and in my panic attacks. He is with my child even when I am not. He never fails, even when I do.

Sometimes his ways have been mysterious. I have been strengthened to do things I thought I couldn't do. I have suddenly known what to say to my child, at the right moment, in the right words, when only a moment before I had been completely bewildered. In moments of utter chaos, I have seen God speak peace into our hearts and calm the storm raging in our home. At times I have failed to pray, failed to obey God's Word, given in to anxiety and fear, and still he has met my sons and me with grace and strength and, yes, joy.

At other times—many, many other times—God has met us through his people. Often our local church has met our needs in the most practical ways. God in his mercy gave us belonging amid the brothers and sisters at Brookwood Baptist Church, and the care of pastors who loved us. Our church has loved us well! He has also surrounded us with Christian neighbors, friends, and coworkers and thrown in other treasures like the praying baseball coach and the Jesus-loving debate teacher. I have no idea how many prayers those good folks have offered on our behalf, but I think if it were possible, they would have worn Jesus out with their intercession. I am convinced that half the times I saw God's mysterious, providential care, someone somewhere was praying for us. I have lifted my eyes to the hills and wondered where my help would come from (Ps. 121), and God has sent a brother or sister in Christ (or sometimes friends who don't know Jesus at all) to come alongside us. God enfolded our family into his family, and they have cared for us.

Is it any wonder we are filled with joy?

I write because I want to encourage you just as God has

encouraged us. God has made himself known to our family and remade us. Like any family, we are still broken by our fallen world and the effects of our sin. We bear scars that reveal just how wounded we are, but we don't want to hide those scars, because they testify to God's faithfulness and steadfast love.

Over the next few chapters, I will return to and expand on the common struggles of single parents. You will

+ hear stories from other families led by a single parent.
+ explore key passages of Scripture that describe how God cares for the single parent and their child.
+ read several examples of how God's church has cared well for single-parent families.
+ find suggestions for how you might love single-parent families well.

Whether or not you are a single parent, this book is for you.

If you are a single parent, I pray you will find encouragement and comfort, knowing that God sees you and hears your prayers. Maybe even more reassuring: God hears the cries of your children, and he responds with the tenderest mercies. He will never leave or forsake you. Families like ours hold a very special place in his care.

If you are not a single parent, I pray that through our testimonies, you will see God's faithfulness, experience more of his deep compassion, and know his character more fully. I pray you will find practical wisdom to guide you in loving single parents and their children well, for the glory of God and the joy of his church.

He is the Father "from whom every family in heaven and on earth receives its true name" (Eph. 3:14–15 GNT), starting with his own family (John 1:12; 1 John 3:1–2; Rom. 8:15–16).

The State of Single-Parent Families and the Church Today

Whoever does the will of my Father in heaven is my brother and sister and mother. (Matthew 12:50)

All the believers were one in heart and mind. No one claimed that any of their possessions was their own, but they shared everything they had. With great power the apostles continued to testify to the resurrection of the Lord Jesus. And God's grace was so powerfully at work in them all that there were no needy persons among them. (Acts 4:32–34)

Thirty percent of families in the US are led by a single parent.[1] Nearly nineteen million children have one parent in the home.[2]

Although roughly thirty verses in the Bible declare how God wants his church to treat widows and the fatherless, by and large the church does not know what to do with families like mine. God declares himself "father to the fatherless, a defender of widows" (Ps. 68:5), yet they are often uneasy members of his body.

These families are the reason I am writing this book and, hopefully, the reason you are reading it.

In the introduction, I gave you a glimpse into some of the challenges our family faced when my husband died. Here, we will broaden the lens to look at single-parent families across the nation.

Important Things to Know about Single-Parent Families

+ Thirty percent of single-parent families live below the poverty line. "Children in poverty are more likely to have physical, mental and behavioral health problems, disrupted brain development, shorter educational trajectories, contact with the child welfare and justice systems, employment challenges in adulthood and more."[3] About one third of those households are food insecure.[4]
+ Children from single-parent homes are at increased risk of sexual abuse.[5]
+ Children from single-parent families are less likely to graduate from high school and more likely to go to jail or experience teen pregnancy.[6]
+ Children who are raised in single-parent homes are more likely to struggle with academic performance and behavior at school.[7]
+ Children in single-parent homes spend more time on social media and are less likely to have regular family dinners.[8]
+ Black children (64 percent) and American Indian children (49 percent) are more likely to be raised in single-parent families than white children (24 percent) or AAPI children (16 percent). Latino children and multiracial children are at 42 percent and 38 percent, respectively.[9]
+ Single parents are sorely limited in their ability to provide for (in every way) and protect their children.

Single Mothers

Twenty-one percent of families are led by a solo mom, representing over fifteen million children.[10] Poverty disproportionately affects single mothers (as opposed to single fathers); they are five times more likely to experience serious financial deficit than single dads. Statistics concerning the absence of fathers paint a grim picture.[11] In her beautiful book, *Finding My Father: How the Gospel Heals the Pain of Fatherlessness*, Blair Linne writes,

> Fathers are protectors, prayer warriors, lovers, spouses, friends, disciplers, playmates, nurturers, encouragers, evangelists, moral guides, teachers, leaders, models, and providers. Or they are not these things. Either way, their impact is immeasurable. Fathers often engage in a paternal playfulness which imprints important lessons like security, risk, and trust in their children. . . . So when a father is absent—whether it is physically, emotionally, or spiritually—it means that the children and mother suffer, but it also means that the community that they are not a part of and the church that they are not serving suffer too.[12]

What's more, Linne writes, "We know that God views fatherhood as important because it is the primary way that he describes himself."[13] He wants his children to relate to him as Father, but without a human reflection of that fatherhood in the home, a family is vulnerable to instability, poverty, and spiritual confusion. What's more, in Scripture God places responsibility for children first on the shoulders of the father, then on the mother. The absence of a father weighs heavily on both mother and child.

The plight of single mothers and their children does get some attention, both inside and outside the church, although at times that attention is negative, with single mothers receiving the blame for numerous social ills. You can help by recognizing and removing the stigma against single mothers wherever you see it. From examining public policies regarding wage equality and parental leave to inviting single-mom families into your homes and churches, find ways to stand up for these kids and their moms however you can. Lord willing, your local church is a great place to start.

Be aware that in some churches there's a subtle implication that families with single moms are spiritually deficient, as if God would give less grace to a single mother because she is a woman leading the home, not a man. That line of thought is not just degrading to women, it's degrading to the God who made women in his image. The Lord of the universe offers himself as Husband to the single mother (Isa. 54:5). He is more than capable of giving her what she needs to disciple her children. British pastor Stephen Kneale (whose sister is a single mother) writes, "That God expects fathers to be responsible for the spiritual welfare of children at home does not mean that single mothers are bound to raise godless children. . . . God is both sovereign and gracious. Is not God primary in salvation?"[14]

Single Fathers

While most single parents are moms, single fathers and their children are very much present and often unaccounted for. Single father–led households account for about 5 percent of all families, representing 3.5 million children.[15] Support systems for single dads are hard to find, and research about their lives is minimal. Because they generally don't struggle financially in the same way single moms do, single dads don't get much attention from anyone.

But they need it. After adjusting for other risk factors, the medical journal *Lancet* found that single fathers' mortality risk was more than two times higher than that of other parents.

Research uncovered a number of factors, including unhealthy eating, binge drinking, stress, grief, and poor social support. Single dads were more likely to be widowed or divorced than single mothers (because single moms are more often never-married).[16] Overall, men struggle less financially, but more relationally. One single dad I interviewed was able to hire a full-time nanny for his toddler when his wife died in an accident, but after his church cared for him in his bereavement, he began to feel "weird" when he was at church and suspected they felt "weird" about him too. It soon became easier not to go at all.

All that information may read like a bunch of numbers, disconnected from any real people you know. Let's get back to the one that means most: nineteen million children are growing up in homes with one parent. That's nineteen million kids who, through no fault of their own, live in a family that doesn't look the way a family is "supposed" to look. That's a whole lot of children who desperately need the love of Jesus and his family and a whole lot of weary, worried parents who need the support of the local church. But we don't make it easy for them.

The American Church Is Designed for the Nuclear Family

The American church is a very married place. It's the old analogy of the fish not noticing the water it swims in because it doesn't know anything else, but unmarried people in the church know it well: whether spoken or unspoken, the understanding is that marriage is—or should be—the goal of every Christian adult. A wedding doesn't just solemnize and celebrate the covenant relationship between a man and wife, it also represents their graduation into the grown-up life of the church. Becoming "uncoupled" (to use Gwyneth Paltrow's term) in the church at best means you don't fit anymore and at worst means you have failed. The Sunday school classes, the programs, the family retreats—all are designed for married parents and their kids. Even the best parenting workshops, books, and podcasts almost always fail to mention that single parents even exist. (Remember, *one in four families . . .*)

However, the life of a single-parent family is dramatically different from the life of a two-parent family. Everything from finances to chores to bath time to staying up for curfew falls on one person, who is perpetually exhausted and finite. When everything in the life and language of the church implies that families are led by couples, the single parent implicitly does not belong, nor does their child. To complicate matters, church leaders are almost always married (or, rarely, single and childless).

As a single-parent family, my boys and I no longer fit the Christian family mold, which assumes two parents because that's the way God designed families. Certainly, God knew what he was doing. The job of raising children is too big for one person. (Wise parents know it takes more than a couple to raise a child, it takes a church.) By God's grace, he gave my family a church that cared for us personally and intentionally, but as much as they loved us, being at church was still a painful reminder of what our family had lost and the ways we no longer fit in. For many newly single parents and their children, already wounded by the absence of the missing parent, that pain is enough to cause them to leave their church home or stop attending church altogether.

Researchers Jim Davis and Michael Graham investigated who exactly is leaving church, and why. They found that the second most important factor in the decision to stop attending church was a major shift in family structure, including divorce, remarriage, unwed pregnancy, loss of a spouse, or other family change. In an interview, Jim Davis commented that "the American church has tended to work best for those who fit the 'American path':

marriage, then children after marriage. If you get off that path, the American church doesn't work as well for you, which is really sad because if you go back to the early church, the people church worked best for were the disenfranchised."[17]

Churches may excel at outreach, but single-parent families don't need to be outside the church, they need to be enfolded and known, close to the hearts of their church family. Leaders may design excellent programs and provide for material needs, but they may not know how uncomfortable it can be for the single parent and their child to sit in the pews surrounded by intact families. The very place God ordained to help widows and orphans can be a very hard place for the single parent and their child to belong.

A friend told me of his neighbor, a single mom with two children. She worked long hours to provide and was often exhausted and lonely. Talking with this woman in her yard one day, my friend asked if her church ever invited her to participate in any of the women's fellowship events. She avoided his eyes as she admitted yes, they always invited her, but she never went. She couldn't afford to hire a babysitter.

The next day he called her church and told the women's ministry director the situation. She was surprised to hear there was a problem; the church could pay a babysitter so the single mom could attend. Several issues come to light through this story:

1. The church did not know how tight money was for this single mom because no one knew her well.
2. The single mother didn't know about the funds. Perhaps she was ashamed of her need; perhaps she was too proud to ask for help. Either way, poor communication kept her and her children distant from their church family.
3. For single parents who work long days, leaving the children at night is far more complicated than it is for a

married parent. The single parent may feel too tired, too busy, or even guilty for leaving. Those who share custody often feel they can't spare time away when their child is in their home.

4. It is natural for single moms to be invited to women's events and single dads to events for men. But are there adult events at your church that are not specifically for married couples or childless singles? The church is the ideal place for single parents to develop God-honoring, appropriate, meaningful friendships across gender lines, and these are the types of friendships the whole church needs.

5. I can't say this strongly enough: although the majority of custodial single parents are moms, single parenting is not a women's issue, it's a family of God issue. Millions of single dads need the church desperately. And half the children raised in single-parent homes are boys.

Finally, churches need single-parent families. Regardless of how a single parent came to be a single parent—whether through personal sin, the sins of another, or the consequences of living in a fallen world—Jesus came for the needy, not for those who have it all together. Families like mine are "weaker vessels," needier than average in some respects but, in God's eyes, worthy of his special honor and care. His power and love and tenderness are made manifest in our families *because* of our need. We bear witness to the living God moving through our homes in power and grace. We, alongside our children, have a testimony that the church needs to hear because all families are in a very real sense "broken" by sin, even if the parents' marriage is intact. This side of glory, there's no such thing as an "unbroken" family. In our particular brokenness, single-parent families bless the church by living out the dependence that makes us strong in Christ.

Single-Parent Stories Matter, and They Don't Matter

When I make a new friend who's married, I love to ask how he or she met their spouse. You can tell a lot about a person by the way they tell that story: the details they share, the affection in their voice, and the laughter that accompanies that memory years later all help me get a sense of who that person is and what matters to them. A couple's meet-cute (or not-so-cute) forms a line in their family's unique fingerprint.

The story of how a single parent came to be a single parent is as unique and personal as a fingerprint and, almost without exception, full of great suffering. We will look at four kinds of single-parent stories, in order of most common to least common.

Divorce creates the majority of single-parent families. These families carry stories of abandonment, abuse (mental, emotional, and physical), addiction, infidelity, incarceration, financial ruin, and mental illness, among other tragedies. Sometimes the story of divorce is a long, slow erosion of affection into hostility or indifference. No one emerges from divorce unscathed, least of all the children.

It is not our objective here to debate grounds for biblical divorce or determine how any church should respond to a couple contemplating divorce. Scripture clearly teaches that God wants married people to stay married, yet 40 to 50 percent of married couples eventually file for divorce, and hundreds of thousands of those couples have children in the home when they do.[18] Regardless of why the couple splits up or who is at fault, divorcing couples lose intimacy, companionship, identity, belonging (both at home and in their various communities), cherished hopes for the future, and their close connection to their child's other parent, not to mention social connections and essential support, financial and otherwise. The list of losses goes on and on. Divorce is by definition excruciating. As one single father said, even though his divorce was "amicable, it still felt like a limb had been cut off."

We must also consider the children. In his excellent book *The Children of Divorce: The Loss of Family as the Loss of Being*, Andrew Root (who was an adult when his own parents divorced) describes the ways in which kids whose parents divorce experience a crisis of identity. The child was conceived in a love that no longer exists, calling into question the very foundation and cause of his or her being in the world. Because of the depth of their loss, "actions must be taken," writes Root, "not only to secure emotional and economic stability, but also . . . to secure the child's being in a community of suffering love."[19] In other words, there is no better place than the church for these families to find love and care in their need.

And yet we often don't welcome divorced families with open arms, but rather with a whole lot of questions. While there is a moral dimension to divorce, we must not take it on ourselves to figure out what happened to the marriage and why. As that same single father said, it's not helpful to try to get a read on who was at fault in the divorce. Rather than probing for "who did what," ask, "How has divorce affected you?" Asking about the impact of the breakup rather than its causes puts focus on the single parent in front of you and helps you know better how to befriend and care for the family.

I've learned from my conversations with divorced parents that members of the church have unwittingly added to their suffering. When we as Christians fail to love divorced people well, we make it hard for them to come to church. Do we really want to deny that family access to the gospel that will heal them? We are all sinners in need of the gospel of grace. We all need a local church body to receive, experience, and offer that grace in fellowship with other believers.

Pregnancy outside of marriage has increased exponentially over the last several decades. It's always astonishing to hear public figures (or anyone, for that matter) speak disparagingly of women who carry unexpected pregnancies to term. If the church is serious about eradicating abortion, we must double down in our efforts to care for women who make the courageous choice to raise their babies.

Imagine if a woman, finding herself pregnant and alone, found a home—a real family—within the church for her and her baby.[20] Imagine the power of their testimony if, twenty years later, mother and child declared that the church welcomed them with joy and belonging and remain committed to their family.

No, it is not God's plan for children to be conceived outside of marriage. But as John Piper says, "It is crucial that every Christian and every church make clear that any stigma to pregnancy outside marriage is because the pregnancy signifies previous sin, not because the pregnancy is sin."[21] We must never confuse the sin with either the pregnancy or the child.[22] "No one needs to feel, no woman needs to feel, no family needs to feel that, because the child originated in a sinful act, if it did, God cannot make this child great. He can."[23] That child was no less hand-knit in her mother's womb, no less created in the image of Almighty God, than any other baby.

I think women who raise their conceived-outside-of-marriage children are heroes. To willingly take on the role of being a single mother before the child is ever born is courageous and brave and self-sacrificing. These women would probably say they are just moms who love their kids, like any other mom.

Adoption is on the rise among single Christian adults in America, so much so that *Christianity Today* ran a cover story, "Christian Singles Aren't Waiting for Marriage to Become Parents," in 2021. The article states that "singles—mostly women —accounted for nearly 30 percent of all public adoptions in 2019, taking in more than 19,000 children." Author Kara Bettis writes, "Like other single parents, these single parents by choice often face immense financial and lifestyle challenges. But in evangelical churches, such parents also have to swim against the current of long-held norms around family."[24] But for the growing number of children who need loving homes, thankfully attitudes are changing. More and more foster and adoption agencies are waiving requirements that adoptive parents need to be married, and churches can make a crucial difference by developing close relationships with parent and child. Bettis quotes Sam Allberry:

> Psalm 68 says that God puts the lonely in families. And that's not primarily just talking about a biological nuclear family; it's talking about the people of God. A single person may be thinking, "I'm just a mum or just a dad and I can't do the role of both parents" but actually, with the support of a wider church family, that child should be growing up in a very, very healthy family context. I think it's a great thing for singles to adopt.[25]

Certainly, adoption is at the core of the father-heart of God (1 John 3:1; Rom. 8:15).

Finally, the *death of a parent* creates a single-parent family and changes every member of that family forever. Whether the parent died from a short illness, a prolonged one, or a sudden traumatic event, he or she will never be present with the child again this side of heaven. No more hugs. No more nicknames or shared jokes. No chance to resolve old hurts or get to know each other better, to ask for advice or explanation. The loss devastates the child and the parent left behind. Every single-parent family grapples with heartbreak in some way, but grief shapes these families, and they will need their church family to stick close for years and years.

Looking at the variety of ways single-parent families are formed, you can imagine that their stories matter enormously. No two single-parent families are alike. Their situation will determine how you care for them. One family may be traumatized by violence, another may need support for a difficult parent-child relationship, another may not have money for food or childcare (and some families may have all these struggles and more).

It is equally true that their stories do not matter at all. Regardless of how that family came to be, each person in it is made in the image of God. As a Christ follower and member of God's family, you befriend and care for the single parent and their children no matter what their history looks like. Their story is never yours to evaluate, as if to determine whether they deserve your friendship and support. The same holds true if that single parent is not a believer or a churchgoer, because we are called to love our neighbors.

The stories of single-parent families matter in *how* you care for them, but regardless of how those stories unfolded, *you must care for them.* Loving single-parent families is nonnegotiable for Christians, and yet single parents don't always feel welcome at church.

The Single-Parent Self-Justification Shuffle

Ask yourself: "When I meet a single parent for the first time, do I have to conceal my curiosity? Do I cast about for tactful ways to probe?" *How did you come to be a single parent? Have you ever been married? Did you have biblical grounds for your divorce, or did you just get tired of fighting?*

Single parents can see these questions hovering over your head like a cartoon speech bubble, and this tendency to probe makes them very uncomfortable.

As a widower dad who is also a pastor and a writer, Eric Tonjes is forthright about how this scrutiny feels for single parents:

They need you to not be a graceless idiot. I could probably [say this] less harshly, but I'm not going to, because I think some bluntness is deserved. I have had the experience, in several contexts, of doing what I think of as the "single parent self-justification shuffle." Christian strangers realize I'm unmarried with kids, they don't know what I do for a living or my story, and they start asking questions that are transparently trying to determine whether I am one of those "good" single parents or one of the "bad" ones. Whether I'm someone they should pity or someone they should judge.[26]

If we casually but strategically work to uncover the real story about a family's "situation," then we are forgetting one of the basic truths of the Christian faith: apart from Christ, "there is no one righteous, not even one" (Rom. 3:10). Tonjes again:

> The problem with those questions and the dance is how little of the gospel there is in it. Jesus doesn't care how someone ended up in a hard situation; he simply sees their pain and calls them to Himself. In fact, it is precisely the question of moral justification and "bad" single people that lies behind the Pharisee's judgment of Jesus when the woman washes his feet. (Luke 7:39)[27]

Imagine visiting a new church for the first time. Someone welcomes you warmly. What if that person, knowing you're a sinner because we all are, then asked questions aimed at uncovering what your particular sins are? How would you feel? Defensive, guarded, ashamed, angry, resentful, embarrassed? I doubt you would feel welcomed, and you certainly would not feel loved. What's more, you would likely never go back.

The "self-justification shuffle" Tonjes so aptly describes puts single parents on their guard among Christians. As a single mom,

I feel defensive of my singleness and of my family when I am among people who don't know our story, and you better believe I feel protective of my kids when people wonder why their dad isn't around. As a widow, I have seen Christians visibly relax when they hear my singleness isn't complicated. I didn't do anything "wrong." Our family enjoys privileged status among Christians who know that God is serious about caring for widows and orphans. The fact that even I, with my straightforward story, have felt the shuffle so acutely makes me angry and sad for single parents with more complex stories. The world outside the church often judges single parents far less severely than people inside the church do.

Brothers and sisters, this should not be so. No one should ever walk into church feeling defensive, and yet single parents and their children often do. No wonder people leave the church after a marriage ends or a single woman discovers she's pregnant. No wonder the single-parent families who do come can find it hard to engage. No wonder these families experience acute loneliness even *inside* the church. No wonder single parents can find it hard to explain God's grace to children who have felt the opposite from people who say they follow Jesus.

Scripture and the Single Parent

God not only offers special protection, provision, and care for the widow, the orphan, and the stranger in both the Old and New Testaments, he also commands that his people offer the same.[28] Our treatment of these families demonstrates the quality of our worship: "Religion that God our Father accepts as pure and faultless is this: to look after orphans and widows in their distress and to keep oneself from being polluted by the world" (James 1:27). Hearts that are pure before God love what he loves, and he loves people on the margins. He wants us to recognize that single parents and their children are on the margins of our churches (and in the world). We show him we love him by taking his command seriously.

James gives us a clue about how to start. Keeping ourselves from being "polluted by the world" means in part that we set aside the idols that keep us from caring for people who need us. Looking after someone will always cost time, energy, and money. It will require that we set aside our own agendas for our families and even our churches and open our eyes to the needs of others. Embracing messy families will cost you tears and time in prayer, and it will pry the facade of perfection off your own messy family. To care for the widow and the orphan, we have to take down the idols we have made of our own marriages or our children or our free time or our extra cash, but we can trust God when he says we won't miss them (Gal. 5:1).

Let's look at what God means when he speaks about widows and orphans. He might not define those terms as narrowly as we do:

> The Bible has a much deeper, more rich description for a widow than simply a woman whose husband has died. The Greek word in the New Testament for widow is *chēra*, which means *bereft*. It literally and culturally in the biblical context is a woman bereft of the provision and flourishing that could be provided by a husband or a family. . . . The circumstances that may have left her bereft in a male-dominated world may have been divorce, abandonment, death, imprisonment. . . . To limit widowhood to an identity that is solely based on the death of a husband cuts short the fullness of both the need and the opportunity at hand.[29]

Here K. A. Ellis demonstrates that we should think of the "widow" not simply as a woman whose husband has died but as a woman who is bereft. Bereft means "deprived or robbed of the use of something; lacking something needed, wanted or expected; suffering the death of a loved one; bereaved"[30] Countless cultural factors have contributed to the rise of single-parent families, and we may safely and biblically count divorced, unwed, and abandoned parents among those who deserve the church's special attention.

In her 2018 Gospel Coalition talk, "Loving the Widow," Ellis made the intriguing argument that in Eden, we all, male and female, became spiritual widows and orphans because sin separated us from our Bridegroom and Father.[31] This in no way dilutes the mandate to care for single parents and their kids, but rather reminds us that as humans we share a spiritual condition. We who "once were far away have been brought near by the blood of Christ" (Eph. 2:13). In him we are made family, and family takes care of its own (Acts 4:33–35).

Please don't read these verses about widowhood to mean single fathers have it easy. Widowed fathers and their children are bereft of a wife and mother's care, and her absence is enormous. Emotionally and relationally, their children are equally disadvantaged without a mother as are their peers who don't have a dad around. The single dads I've spoken with humbly recognize their limitations raising children without a wife. Most (at least of those who kept going to church when they became single) tried to find women in their churches and communities who could offer their children female nurturing and discipleship. Single dads desperately need Christian fellowship with other men and with women. Don't overlook these men or their children because you think Scripture doesn't demonstrate their need for the body of Christ.

Talking with Single Parents: What I've Learned

In preparing to write this book, I interviewed dozens of single parents. You'll hear pieces of their stories. Many of the insights here are theirs. My questions were few and simple. I would generally start our conversations by hearing about their children (who doesn't love to talk about their kid?) and then move into asking for the story of their family. I would ask how the church had loved them well and what they wished the church had done differently. Finally, I asked what they found to be the hardest part of being a single parent, how God had loved their families well, and what they would say to readers—single parents and church members—if they were the ones writing this book.

As unique as each parent was, these interviews generally shared three characteristics that warrant our attention.

1. **Sharing their stories was hard.** Nearly every person I spoke to was reluctant at first to talk about their experience. Their histories were painful and their struggles ongoing. One mom said to me, "You're asking me to open up my biggest failures to you. I'm not sure I want to share all that." In many cases, becoming a single parent was the most agonizing experience of their lives, and the fallout from whatever happened continues to affect everyone in the family. Most single-parent families have known great suffering. We must meet every member of those families with the gentleness of Jesus.

2. All parents long to love and bless their children, and all parents fall short in ways large and small. But single parents know they can't give their kids all the blessings that come with having a mom and a dad in the home, so a **yearning sort of sadness** accompanies their deep love for their children. However, these parents have often had to fight for their children in some real way. Custody battles, financial strain, unhealthy relationships, traumatic events—all of these arouse a parent-love that is fierce, protective, and sacrificial. These parents love their children as intensely as any parent ever could.

3. Nearly every parent commented at the end of the interview, "**No one ever asked me these questions before.**" Let that sink in for a minute. Most of these moms and dads had *never been asked* what it was like to be a single parent or what was hard for them. What hurt most is that no one from their church had ever asked these questions. Many single parents had sought and received counsel from a pastor or friend, but no one from their church had ever approached them to discover how their belonging might be made more comforting and comfortable. Church, we must start asking good questions, paying attention to unique circumstances, and making friends with families led by one parent.

Receive the single parents in your midst as you would anyone who bears the image of the living God. That is to say, welcome them with warmth, affirm their dignity, honor their great love for their children, share your life with them, and invite them to share theirs with you.

No one expresses this more poetically than K. A. Ellis. Where she uses the word *widow*, remember she is speaking about the bereft, which includes the single parent and the child who feels the absence of the other parent like an open wound. The bereft have much to teach us.

I say let the bereft of the world, including the widow, show us the way. How should we love the widow? To encourage the widow is to love her. To empower the widow is to love her. To sit at the feet of the widow and learn, is to love her. And [the bereft] will remind us who we are capable of being: Powerful. Strong. Decisive. Trusting. Teaching. Believing.[32]

one

God's Steadfast Love for the Single Parent and Their Child

"Behold, you are pregnant
and shall bear a son.
You shall call his name Ishmael [meaning "God hears"],
because the LORD has listened to your affliction." . . .

"You are a God of seeing. . . . Truly here I have seen him
who looks after me." (Genesis 16:11, 13 ESV)

Maggie[1] squeezed her eyes shut, then opened them slowly, hoping to read a different result. Committed to celibacy until marriage, she gave in to temptation one time with a guy she didn't even want to date. Now, at age twenty-four, she found herself staring at two pink lines on a pregnancy test.

To complicate matters further, Maggie was in seminary, having just started her first full-time job as a youth minister discipling teens at a church in California. Maggie not only had to tell her boss (her pastor!) she was pregnant, she also had to tell her impressionable students and their parents that she had slept with a man and that the consequences included a child.

But Maggie already loved that child. Because she knew Jesus loved her so deeply that he secured her pardon for sin on the cross, she felt confident in bringing this child into the world and raising him, even as a single mother. What she did not know was how her church would respond.

God Sees Hagar

If we ever wondered how God feels about the lonely single parent, the story of Hagar is our answer. This single mother figures prominently in the life of the great patriarch Abraham. Brought from Egypt as a slave for Abraham's wife Sarah, Hagar lives at the very heart of the establishment of God's covenant with his own people.

When Sarah endures about ten years without holding the promised child in her arms, she conceives instead a plan to make God's promise come true: let Abraham impregnate the young slave girl. According to custom, the child of the slave will belong to Sarah.

Consider Hagar's predicament. She is forced to sleep with her boss, who is not only married but also old. Her mistress sees her as an incubator for God's promised child, a child she plans to take from Hagar and raise as her own. To Abraham and Sarah, Hagar is not a person but an instrument to carry out their personal agenda. It's no wonder Hagar treats Sarah with contempt when she does conceive. She finally has some clout in this lopsided triangle.

Sarah responds to Hagar's insolence by complaining to Abraham, who abdicates responsibility for his unborn child, giving Sarah free rein to do whatever she likes with Hagar. Sarah "deals harshly" with her, to the point that Hagar flees to the wilderness.

In this moment, Hagar is as vulnerable as a person could possibly be. She is a woman in a culture that does not value women. She is a slave, and a foreign one at that. She is penniless and pregnant, with no resources and no support. The people who were supposed to take care of her have made her life unbearable. She is not even part of the chosen race that God will establish through Abraham. No one is coming to help her; no one cares.

Were it not for Abraham's God, Hagar and her unborn child would have died alone in the desert. No one would ever have known her name.

"The angel of the Lord met Hagar at a spring in the desert on the road to Shur and said, 'Hagar, slave of Sarai, where have you come from and where are you going?'" (Gen. 16:7–8 GNT). Hagar does not know Abraham's God. She likely worshiped Egypt's pagan idols if she had any faith at all. Incredibly, the angel of the Lord comes *looking for her*. Her insignificance in the eyes of the world does not render her insignificant in God's sight. She is an outsider in every possible way, and yet he calls her by name and declares her situation: "Hagar, servant of Sarah . . ."

The angel invites her to talk with him. The question he asks her echoes God's question to Adam in the garden: "Where are you?" He cares about her history ("Where have you come from?") and her future ("Where are you going?"). When Hagar admits she is running away from Sarah, the angel instructs her to return to her mistress.

That must have been a hard word for Hagar to hear. Her situation with Abraham and Sarah won't be easy. But the angel's encounter with her meets a need much deeper than a desire for ease or comfort. The angel reveals to Hagar a God who knows, sees, and hears her and her unborn baby. This God is willing to be personally involved and provide for both of them, even naming her son Ishmael, meaning "God hears." The angel tells her that the boy will be a "wild donkey of a man," at odds with everyone around him, but Hagar's boy will live (16:12).

Let's not miss how astounding this encounter must have been

for Hagar. Despised and alone, she is filled with despair so great that she has run away to near-certain death in the desert. There she is met with a heavenly being who knows the intimate details of her life yet treats her with dignity and compassion. This changes everything. She can go back to Sarah, harsh treatment and all, confident that Almighty God has his eye on her. God's provision will not mean an easy life, but as a part of Abraham's household, she will have protection for her boy. Every time she calls her son in to wash up for dinner, she will be reminded that "God hears!"

God Hears Hagar's Son

Hagar's troubles with Sarah don't end. Rather, they reach a boiling point after Isaac, the child of the covenant, is finally born. This time Sarah banishes Hagar into the wilderness with Ishmael.[2] When they run out of water, Hagar's faith in God's promises falters, and she places her son under a bush to die.

Alone and despairing again, Hagar "lifted up her voice and wept" (Gen. 21:16 ESV). The angel speaks to Hagar, graciously declining to rebuke her for doubting God's promises for her son. Instead, he assures her that God not only sees her but has heard Ishmael: "What troubles you, Hagar? Fear not, for God has heard the voice of the boy where he is" (v. 17 ESV).

For me, for Hagar, for any parent, the only thing more wonderful than knowing God sees and cares for *me* is knowing that God sees and cares for *my child*. Hagar's deepest fears and worries for her child have been met with the tender, personal care of Yahweh himself.

Nothing that has been done to Hagar—and she has been poorly treated—disqualifies her or her child from God's protection and provision. What's more, nothing Hagar has done—and she hasn't been blameless—disqualifies her from God's compassion.

In her distress, she even goes so far as to doubt that God's personal, miraculous word to her son will come to pass, and still she has not outsinned God's grace and mercy. As for her son, God will "make a nation" of Ishmael, simply for Abraham's sake, even though Abraham has not been a reliable father.

God's grace overflows to them all: for Hagar and Ishmael, for Abraham and Sarah. Single parent, the same is true for you: God's grace is sufficient for you and your children (2 Cor. 12:9).

What Is It about God, Women, and Wells?

This time God does not send Hagar back to Sarah. Instead, he opens her eyes to a well of water close by, and she gives Ishmael a lifesaving drink (Gen. 21:19). From that time on, "God was with the boy," and he grows up to fulfill all that God had promised (v. 20).

Hagar's well calls to mind another time when God meets a woman at a well. In John 4, Jesus meets a Samaritan woman drawing water and strikes up a conversation. She, too, is an outsider (the text tells us that "Jews do not associate with Samaritans," v. 9), but Jesus knows that her thirst goes far beyond a dry throat. As with Hagar, he is the God who truly *sees* her most intimate circumstances, yet by his actions he dignifies a woman whom everyone else has treated badly. The Samaritan woman has had five husbands and currently is with man number six, but none of this deters Jesus from offering her "living water. . . . Whoever drinks the water I give them will never thirst" (vv. 10, 14). Before their conversation is over, he confirms that he is the Messiah she has been waiting for (v. 26), and she is so thrilled that she can't stop talking about him in town.

What does this mean for single parents? It means Jesus does

not wait for us to be "insiders" to come to us. He knows our most personal history. And yet our sin does not prevent him from offering his salvation, his friendship, his love, and his protection. We don't know if the woman at the well is a mother; what we do know is that, like Hagar, like all of us, she needs the living water that only Jesus can give. It is his delight to seek out and provide for both women, regardless of what they have done, regardless of what has been done to them.

What This Means for the Church

The first thing that the gospel tells us about our nature as humans is that "all have sinned and fall short of the glory of God" (Rom. 3:23). Every one of us needs the living water Jesus offers. While our sin might not have resulted in a pregnancy or a divorce or some visible life circumstance, our sin has serious consequences too.

None of us has room to judge the single parent in our midst. Instead, "welcome one another as Christ has welcomed you" (Rom. 15:7 ESV)—as another person who needs living water.

If you are married or single without a child, be aware that single parents often fear being judged at church. This fear can drive single parents away from the church, regardless of whether the judgment is real or perceived. To love well, Christians must fight a tendency to judge those in difficult straights. Ray Ortlund writes,

> Every personal suffering has a social dimension, as others look on and invariably form opinions. Suffering brings temptation to both the sufferer and to the observer. The sufferer is tempted to give up on God. The observer is tempted to point his finger with smug, self-serving thoughts and words: "This is all your fault, of course." . . . Our minds dredge up these

thoughts not really because we are confident in ourselves, but because we are uneasy about ourselves and therefore threatened by the suffering of another.[3]

God forbid we add to the suffering of a parent or child by casting blame in a misguided attempt to justify ourselves. God forbid that our judgment tempt anyone anywhere to give up on God or his church.

The tendency to judge means that ministering to single parents begins in your prayer life. You may not be aware of any judgment, but have the humility to ask God to search your heart and deal with any judgment that's there. Judgment can be sneaky: it can take the form of finding smug security in regular date nights with your spouse, or in continued purity when you are single. Single parents can be oversensitive, feeling judged where they are not, so make sure you don't have a whiff of it on you. Don't make it easy for the single mom or dad to avoid their church family.

Being a single parent is hard enough without feeling the burden of disapproval at church. Melissa LaCross shares that after becoming an unwed mom in her late teens, "most people in my larger community continued to relate to me with awkwardness—or silence."[4] John Greco recalls, "For months after my divorce, it felt like I was wearing a scarlet 'D' in church."[5] Children sense their parents' discomfort, and it affects them. Bible teacher Jen Wilkin says that after her parents divorced when she was eight, "we spent our childhood moving from church to church . . . because when you are a divorced woman in a church context, you are a square peg in a round hole. It is very hard to fit in."[6]

Many factors, which we will examine in this book, make single parents "square pegs" in church contexts. The experience of facing judgmentalism is one we can do something about.

Tread this ground carefully and prayerfully. Single parents come to the place of solo parenting in many ways: divorce, death, adoption, pregnancy outside of marriage (wanted and unwanted), incarceration, abandonment, and the list goes on. We listen to their stories not to evaluate them for transgressions but because we care. The particulars do matter because personal details will let you know where the family has been wounded and what they might need. One family may be struggling to pay for shoes. Another may be securing a restraining order. Still another looks perfectly stable on the outside, but inside parent and child are sliding into the darkest depression.

You can learn these details when you start by being friends. Don't keep your distance. If a single parent goes to your church or is a workplace acquaintance, reach out. Share a coffee with a single mom on a cold bleacher at a soccer game, or invite a father and his kids to come over for Sunday lunch, whether or not they went to church with you. Hagar felt known because she was seen and heard. Jesus was able to minister to the Samaritan woman because he knew her story. He saw her sin and her pain, and he offered her himself, living water.

Maggie, Her Son, and the Church

When Maggie became pregnant, she was mature enough in her relationship with Jesus to trust that he would provide for her and her little boy. Secure in his love, and well supported by the church where she worked, she was able to own her sin and be free from condemnation. She chose to move across the country to be closer to family who had the flexibility to help care for her baby, but her church in California sent her off with a baby shower.

By God's grace, when Maggie moved, she found a new church that has embraced her and her son. That church has treated Maggie and her son like any other family. On the one hand, she appreciated that warm welcome, but on the other hand, she wishes someone in the church had thought to ask her how they might support her as a single mother raising a son without his dad. No one ever acknowledged that her son needed male role models in the absence of his dad, or that he was left out of father-son events. Her parents and siblings stepped in to meet practical needs and relational connections that the church didn't offer. Now that her son is a teenager and she is on the cusp of marriage, she wonders how the church will support the blended family she and her husband will create, but she hopes in Christ for her family's future.

If we want moms and dads to be committed to their child's spiritual life, as Maggie was even before her child was born, we will treat all unwed parents with the same grace and commitment that Maggie's churches gave her. If we want those parents to find a home in a local church, we will embrace them with genuine warmth, learning the particulars of their stories so we can love them, not so we can judge them. And we will open our hearts wide to welcome their beloved children.

— *two* —

God's Sufficiency in Our Not-Enoughness

I lift up my eyes to the mountains—
where does my help come from?
My help comes from the LORD,
the Maker of heaven and earth. (Psalm 121:1–2)

Heather is a smart, well-educated woman with a good job. Her husband also worked, so there was no reason to worry that the two of them wouldn't be able to provide what their son and daughter needed.

But when emotional abuse in her marriage became unbearable, she knew that providing for her children included protecting them from their father. Stripped of the future she had hoped for, Heather did not have the words to pray. She knew only that as the Spirit was interceding for her "through wordless groans" (Rom. 8:26), her family's neediness was just beginning.

Heather's wordless groans were only the first of countless times she would come up short in her nearly thirteen years as a single mom, the first of countless times she would need to rely on God to provide for their needs. Finances were often tight. She had enough to pay the bills as long as nothing extra came along, but of course something always does. When she discovered rotten siding on her house, she had no way to cover the $1,700 of repairs she needed. Imagine her surprise—and joy—when her boss called her into his office to tell her she'd been granted a random midyear bonus that, after taxes, would cover the repairs with $100 to spare.

Without her desperation as a single mom, Heather is convinced she would never have known God as her provider and sustainer. Today she sees that the Lord provides *everything*—that job, that boss, those prayers from the Spirit—and she is finding some relief from the burden of self-sufficiency and enjoying a greater rest and freedom.

Joe and his wife were high school sweethearts who came to faith in a college ministry. But when their son was thirteen, Joe's wife announced she no longer believed in God and was leaving the church and their family. Joe recognized instantly that discipling his son to know Jesus was now his responsibility alone. "All Christian parents feel their spiritual inadequacy whether they are married or not," he said. "I get that. That's not in any parent's control. But feeling that weight—I am *the* spiritual presence, teacher, provider, authority, caretaker, whatever—all the responsibilities, I felt it profoundly." For Joe, the stress of this responsibility proved to be the greatest fallout of the divorce, the worry keeping him awake at night. Not having grown up in a Christian home himself, he had always struggled to know how to talk with his son about Jesus, and now he had to figure it out alone.

Leaning into their church family became essential to Joe. His small group, comprised of adults of all ages, single and married, included children whenever the group met so that Joe could bring his son too. The boy ended up with a whole group of adults who knew and loved him well, and over time, his son grew to love both Jesus and his church.

God Provides for the Widow of
Zarephath and Her Son (and Elijah)

Throughout the centuries when the Bible was written, widows were among the most vulnerable citizens of any community. Although they labored from sunup past sundown to survive and provide for their families in their difficult agrarian economy, they were not allowed to own property. In fact, women had no legal rights at all. A woman whose husband died was bound for certain destitution, with no reliable means to protect or feed her family.

Given the poverty most widows endured, Elijah would have been astonished when God told him to go to Zarephath to find a certain widow whom God had commanded to provide for him.

The entire region has been suffering from a drought for months, brought on by the prophetic judgment of the Lord (Deut. 11:16–17; 1 Kings 17:1, 7). Initially God sends Elijah to live by the Brook Cherith, where he enjoys twice-daily meals served by ravens (so maybe it won't be such a stretch for him to believe that a widow is going to feed him). According to Leviticus 11, ravens were unclean, unsuitable for eating, and yet God uses them to deliver dinner. Then again, widows were recipients of God's generosity, not providers of it (Deut. 14:29). God is upending expectations in every corner of this story, teaching us about who he is and how we relate to other people.

When the brook dries up, God sends Elijah to the widow. He finds her gathering sticks near the gate of the gentile city of Zarephath and asks her for a drink of water. Considering the drought conditions, water is a precious commodity, and her willingness to serve confirms for Elijah that this is the widow God sent him to find. He asks her to bring him some bread too, but drought has led to famine, and she has almost nothing to give.

Imagine what this single mom might have been thinking at this point. She might have been a generous soul who was sorry she didn't have bread to share. Or perhaps her suffering—the loss of her husband, the endless drought, their grinding poverty, her inability to feed her son—had made her bitter. She doesn't yet know Elijah's God; maybe she thinks this wilderness prophet is crazy. (I would.) She seems resigned to starvation, planning for her last meal with her son: "As surely as the Lord your God lives . . . I don't have any bread—only a handful of flour in a jar and a little olive oil in a jug. I am gathering a few sticks to take home and make a meal for myself and my son, that we may eat it—and die" (1 Kings 17:12).

Elijah responds, "Don't be afraid" (v. 13). Easier said than done for a despairing widow facing the imminent death of her beloved son. It's not easy for us either: the single dad watching his child leave for the weekend with an unreliable mother, the single mom hearing the pop of gunfire across the street at midnight. The dangers are real, and our fears often are too.

Yet "don't be afraid" is often God's first word to one who has every reason to be terrified, every need to stand courageous on God's Word and character. It's his word to us too, not because there aren't good reasons to be afraid but because there are—and because God's love, strength, and power are always greater than whatever those reasons to be afraid might be. His "don't be afraid" is never dismissive of our concerns. Rather, God calls us to trust that he will provide in ways we don't yet see because he deeply loves and cares for our children and for us.

The widow of Zarephath will learn this firsthand. Elijah asks her to make him a cake, serving him first, and then she will see the Lord make good on a promise: the flour and the oil she has been conserving so anxiously will not run out until the drought is over (v. 14). As Old Testament scholar and commentator Dale Ralph Davis puts it, God seems to say, "Give me everything you have [v. 13] and I will give you everything you need [v. 14]."[1]

So she does, and God does.

Every single morning after, this little trio had enough to eat. Just as God gave daily manna to sustain the Israelites in the wilderness, he gave the widow, her son, and Elijah food for the day. Living handout-to-mouth was probably not what the widow wanted. Most parents prefer to go to bed with a reasonably well-stocked pantry, knowing there will be breakfast on the table for the kids tomorrow. Cooking up the contents of the jar of flour and the jug of oil each day must have felt risky and possibly even foolish to the widow, and yet she discovered in the most practical way that God's mercies are new every morning (Lam. 3:22–23).

Davis reminds us that it's crucial not to expect God to provide for us in the exact ways he provided for Elijah and the widow. As we saw in Heather's story, our families will certainly endure seasons of need. After all, there were many widows—and married folks—in Zarephath who suffered during the drought and did not have a prophet with a promise handy. God may not provide what we think we want, or even what we think we need, but he will never forsake his children. Because of this, we persevere in prayer and in believing that "God will meet all your needs according to the riches of his glory" (Phil. 4:19). Our calling, as Davis says, is to "go on worshipping Yahweh though I never meet ravens bearing gifts."[2]

Let's call a spade a spade: believing God will meet our needs is hard. Watching our kids struggle with lack, knowing we can't provide all we want to give, is truly painful for any parent. Single parents experience this helpless insufficiency in some form or another every single day. You can't afford the coveted piano lessons (or the power bill); there's only one driver for all the carpools; you don't know how to teach your son to shave; there's no mom to plait her hair. Worshiping Yahweh in these moments often takes the form of honest lament in prayer. After my husband died, I asked God, "Your Word says, 'My God will meet all your needs according to the riches of his glory in Christ Jesus.' Don't children need their father? Don't my boys need their dad? How is it possible that you are keeping this promise when he's not here?"

Because God's Word is true, then in the mysterious providence of God it must also be true that because they have Christ, my children don't need their father.

Want him? Yes. Every day for the rest of our lives, my children and I want him to be here. We desperately wish that Jeff had not died. In the same way, the absence of a second parent or the absence of a marriage binding parents together will affect you and your children.

But in Christ, we have everything we need to raise our children. And our kids have everything they need to grow up strong in the Lord: "His divine power has given us *everything we need* for a godly life through our knowledge of him who called us by his own glory and goodness" (2 Peter 1:3, emphasis added).

This verse is not a religious platitude, a truth we toss lightly at suffering people. This promise is a literal lifeline for parents who can't see how God is meeting their family's needs and beg him daily to reveal how he is at work in their desperation.

Sometimes it seems incredible, even laughable, that God would ask us to believe our families have what we need in Christ when our lives seem stripped bare by loss. This is the work of believing (John 6:29), to wake up every morning like the widow did and expect God to feed your wobbly, trembling faith with a spiritual meal hearty enough to get you through the day. We pray for the specifics, like money for school supplies or someone to help with a troubled child, and we trust God with the answer, even if it doesn't arrive in the way or at the time we hoped it would. His mercies take many forms, sometimes forms we don't at first recognize as mercies, but they are real and inexhaustible.

What This Means for the Church

The body of Christ has much to learn from the relationship between Elijah and the widow of Zarephath.

Like Hagar, our widow from 1 Kings is an outsider, a gentile who does not initially know the God of Elijah. She hails from Sidon, the hard-core pagan nation that brought us Jezebel, the queen whose name is synonymous with idolatrous evil. Yet God chooses this widow, rather than any of the available Israelite widows or wives, to provide for Elijah. Jesus points this out to those at the synagogue in Nazareth when he preaches his first sermon, much to the fury of the assembled crowd (Luke 4:26, 28). The religious elite want Jesus to be as exclusive as they are, and yet God not only singles out a gentile widow for his special attention and mercy but bypasses the insider Israelites to do so and, in the process, powerfully demonstrates his love for those "outside" religious and cultural norms.

God is on the lookout to give grace to whoever will acknowledge they need it, and we all need it, whether we know it or not (Isa. 53:6). The Israelites are certainly not disqualified; Elijah represents the greatest among them, and he is grateful for God's grace even when it arrives in the talons of dirty birds. We must not become like Jesus's audience in Nazareth, comfortable in outward displays of religion like our churchgoing, committee-leading, and tithing. Attending church doesn't necessarily mean we are aware of our need for God's grace. This is one reason God commands us to care for the marginalized in the first place: not because we are secure in our marriages, our families, or our religious habits and practices but because their need reminds us of our own (Deut. 24:21–22).

All three of the hungry people in our story—Elijah, the widow, and her son—receive what they need from our gracious God. In the case of the ravens, God's provision is supernatural; in the case of the cake the widow bakes for Elijah, the provision comes through relationship between two people committed to obeying God. In the case of the replenishing flour and oil, God's provision comes through supernatural means *and* relationship— their relationship with each other and with God.

In other words, while God is always the one who provides, he most often meets needs through relationships. And relationship is what church members have to offer single parents and their kids.

You're Making Friends, Not Taking On Projects

Single parents are not ministry opportunities. They hunger to be seen and known, to have and to be real friends. Most feel desperately out of place at church until someone befriends them. That friendship means they need you to understand their family's unique hardships. Refuse to look at their family as an opportunity for your ministry. They don't want your pity, but they do need your compassion. As one divorced mom pointed out to me, single-parent families are not problems to be solved. She laughingly recalled the elderly woman who came up to her in church saying, "Oh, you poor dear, I am so glad you came to church!" She patted this woman on the hand and said, "Well, I am so glad *you* came too!"

Every person in the church needs every other person in the church. In teaching about Elijah's friendship with the widow, pastor John Lin of Redeemer Presbyterian Church Downtown in New York City says, "The God of the Bible works in the lives of people who are not like you, not like me, not like us, and in fact you need people who are not like you . . . to see how God truly works." Otherwise, our view of God stays "one-dimensional: You have to know all the people in whom God works to fully grasp how God works."[3]

The single parent you befriend has something to offer you too: a vision of how God works in their life. Single parents live on the edge of not having enough every single day. In truth, this is the position we are all in, all the time, only our spouses and bank accounts and air conditioning and 401(k)s make that easy to forget. We are all one stock market crash or diagnosis or fill-in-the-blank disaster away from realizing how vulnerable we are to losing everything we rely on to be "enough" for our children.

I write these words not to scare anyone but to remind us that some people in our churches and communities live in lack every day. Single parents are some of those people. Their families are especially dependent on the daily mercy and grace of God, and they know it. If you get to know them, their lives will testify to the steadfast love and faithfulness of the God they rely on, all day every day. You will see embodied long-suffering that is empowered by the Father who has suffered long with their family. You will see how the power and love of God have "[satisfied their] needs in a sun-scorched land," transforming their homes into "well-watered garden[s]" (Isa. 58:11).

Where God is at work, fruit will grow in barren places. Remember that Elijah asks *the widow* for help. It's a noteworthy reversal of the usual design God has for his church to provide for more vulnerable members. Out of her extreme poverty, this widow gives what God asks. In feeding Elijah, she is fed by God. Just remember that God initiates the request, not Elijah. God asks her to feed Elijah because he plans to provide what she needs in order to do it. God works his miracle through this widow, graciously drawing her into his story of redemption in the world.

How to Invite Single Parents to Serve

When we suggest that single parents serve in our churches, we let God prompt the request. We don't rob single parents of opportunities to serve where they can, because they need the blessing of giving every bit as much as other members do (Acts 20:35). It's God's design for all believers to care for each other, and no one is exempt. At the same time, recognize that for single parents, time and resources are almost always very limited. Don't assume single parents can't help out, but don't burden them by assuming they can.

In the course of my interviews, one subject came up often: teaching Sunday school. The Sunday school hour is particularly tender for single parents. After they drop off their children in their respective classes, single parents often have nowhere to go.

As one parent observed, "Single parents are not single people." The single adult class is probably not a fit for the single mom or dad. However, classes full of couples—even if marriage is not explicitly stated anywhere in the class description—often feel awkward.

If you've been kind and thoughtful enough to notice the single parent's Sunday school dilemma, be careful about assuming you'll "solve their problem" (there's that mentality again) by enlisting that single parent to teach. Several of the single parents I spoke with taught Sunday school, but often with mixed feelings. They appreciated being given a place to belong. They felt the honor in being asked. But nearly all of them were reluctant to refuse and exhausted by the extra responsibility. One divorced mother appreciated the vote of confidence in her spiritual maturity that being a Sunday school teacher represented; even so, she felt burdened by being asked to give more, when often she came to church depleted from raising two young children alone and working her full-time job. After pouring herself out for others all week, she needed rest and spiritual nourishment.

Yes, all of us come to church needing to be spiritually fed, and yes, God calls teachers, even during times of their lives when it's not particularly convenient to teach. But proceed carefully in the ways you invite single parents to serve in your church, respecting the tremendous burdens they already carry. Know your single parents well, and pray about it. Together you can discern whether God is calling that single mom or dad to take on extra responsibilities while the kids are still at home.

The God Who Provides What Our Families Need

Wendy lay alone in her bed, afraid she would die. A year after her divorce she had received a cancer diagnosis, and one long night her suffering came to a head. Her two young sons were asleep down the hall, she was too sick to call for help, and she "felt utterly alone in the world facing death."[4]

God brought to mind a friend who was often awake in the night. She managed to call the friend, who called an ambulance, came to the house, and stayed with Wendy's children for two days while Wendy was in the ICU. Wendy says, "At the time I was too weak to fully grasp how God had seen my affliction and cared for me and my children when I felt I was about to be snuffed out. But later, I marveled at the God who really did see me, who really did hear my prayers."[5] He brought a willing person to do for this single mom what she couldn't do for herself. Wendy was not "enough," but she didn't have to be, because God, and his church, were.

three

God's Courage in Our Fear

Do not fear, for I have redeemed you;
  I have summoned you by name; you are mine.
When you pass through the waters,
  I will be with you;
and when you pass through the rivers,
  they will not sweep over you.
When you walk through the fire,
  you will not be burned;
  the flames will not set you ablaze. (Isaiah 43:1–2)

"M ommy, is everything all right?" Renee's son piped up from the back seat. Driving her son home from daycare, Renee was so consumed with worry over her bad day at work that she wasn't even listening to her son's happy chatter. And now she had to figure out a truthful, age-appropriate answer to his simple question.

Every day since her divorce, Renee has worried she will be fired. Fear clouds her mind from the time she hurries her son through his breakfast (can't be late) into the evening, when she hurries through bedtime to get it all done. Renee respects her boss, but she has seen a couple of coworkers fired and is terrified it will happen to her. She can't figure out whether her fears are justified, but either way, she can't stop replaying thoughts of how quickly she and her son would lose everything if she lost her job. "There's no buffer," she says. "I don't have backup." She feels God urging her to trust him, but it's hard when she has never known what financial security feels like.

I clenched the steering wheel so tightly my hands ached. Periodically, I would wipe the sweat off my palms onto my shorts. I was afraid they would become too slippery to keep control of the car.

About a year and a half after my husband died, I took my boys on a vacation. Our time together was not peaceful. The boys bickered endlessly, everyone wanted to do something different, and a vacation was no fun without Dad. Now, driving back to Boise on two-lane rural roads in the foothills, I trembled in the grip of a full-blown panic attack. None of my kids were old enough to drive. It was up to me to get us safely to the airport.

My kids were terrified, I was a mess, and there was no faking fine to convince them otherwise. But in his mercy, God brought Psalm 121 to mind, probably because I was driving through literal mountains in dire need of help. I had one of my sons read the psalm on repeat, out loud, the whole two hours. I clung to those words as tightly as I clung to the steering wheel:

> I lift up my eyes to the mountains—
>   where does my help come from?
> My help comes from the LORD,
>   the Maker of heaven and earth. . . .
>
> The LORD will keep you from all harm—
>   he will watch over your life;

> The LORD will watch over your coming and going
> both now and forevermore. (vv. 1–2, 7–8)

The God who was powerful enough to make the heavens and the earth was powerful enough to overcome my weakness and get us safely to the airport. The panic did not pass. I did not stop shaking until long after we'd returned the rental car. The help I received wasn't as outwardly dramatic as the widow's replenished jar of flour, nor did we cruise into town singing along to a Spotify playlist. Nevertheless, God delivered us and we were safe.

God Encourages Joshua

As I said, two months after my husband died, I started a journal. The first verse I copied into that journal was Deuteronomy 31:7–8:

> Then Moses summoned Joshua and said to him in the presence of all Israel, "Be strong and courageous, for you must go with this people into the land that the LORD swore to their ancestors to give them, and you must divide it among them as their inheritance. The LORD himself goes before you and will be with you; he will never leave you nor forsake you. Do not be afraid; do not be discouraged."

What a moment! Standing at the edge of history, Joshua is about to lead Israel into the fulfillment of a centuries-old promise. They will take possession of the territory that God promised Abraham, a lush land overflowing with milk and honey, where God will establish them as a nation. Finally, Israel is going home.

In the presence of this vast audience, Moses lays the mantle of leadership on the shoulders of his right-hand man, Joshua.

Joshua has faithfully served alongside Moses ever since Egypt. About forty years earlier, when Moses sent twelve men to spy out the land, it was no surprise that he chose Joshua to scout it out. It was also no surprise when Joshua's report was a favorable one— the land was as fertile as it was beautiful—but the tribes who already lived there intimidated the other spies. Joshua and Caleb alone understood that because the Lord was with them, Israel did not have to fear what lay ahead (Num. 14:9). You know the story: because they have faith in their God, Joshua and Caleb will be the only Israelites still alive to enter the promised land when God finally allows the people in (see Numbers 13–14).

So in our passage from Deuteronomy, the time has finally come for Israel to move into their new homeland. For Joshua, there will be one crucial difference from the scenario forty years earlier: Moses won't be there. For all the years of leadership Joshua has under the belt of his tunic, Moses has been right beside him. Moses, who spoke with Yahweh "face to face, as one speaks to a friend" (Ex. 33:11). Moses, with his decades of wisdom and experience leading this rowdy nation. Moses, who surely felt like a really great dad to Joshua. Now Joshua will be leading alone.

To be clear, my husband was not Moses, and my three young boys weren't a nation of "stiff-necked" nomads aiming to settle down. (Though they are definitely stiff-necked, as is their mother.) But Joshua's fear resonated with me. As a leader under Moses, Joshua spoke boldly of trusting their ever-present Lord. Leading without Moses, Joshua needed repeated reminders that God would never leave him. As a mom alongside my husband, I felt secure (even smug) in our traditional biblical two-parent family, confident that together we could do a good job raising our boys. Now the leadership—spiritual and otherwise—I had shared with Jeff rested solely with me. I needed to hear the refrain God spoke over Joshua repeatedly: "I will be with you; I will never leave you nor forsake you. Be strong and courageous" (Josh. 1:5–6).

In the first chapter of the book of Joshua, God speaks some version of that refrain over Joshua *three times* in the first *nine verses*. We've already seen that it's a carryover from Deuteronomy, that the Lord has repeatedly told Moses to "encourage" Joshua (Deut. 1:38; 3:28). Clearly, Joshua is afraid, even terrified, at the prospect of leading these unpredictable people into a hostile take-over of some prime real estate. Let's look at the sequence of God's encouragement in Joshua's panicked moment, because we need to hear the same messages from God that Joshua did.

1. **Changed circumstances:** *"Moses my servant is dead"* *(Josh. 1:2)*. That's the situation in its starkest terms. God says it because for some reason Joshua needed to hear it. Going forward, Joshua will live a different life without Moses by his side. Their season of working together is over.

2. **Unchanging grace:** *"I will give you every place where you set your foot, as I promised Moses"* *(v. 3)*. No matter what happens or how out of control a situation seems, God's promises are stronger than death, and he will continue to pour out grace on the people he loves.

3. **Steadfast presence:** *"As I was with Moses, so I will be with you; I will never leave you nor forsake you"* *(v. 5)*. God will go with them, and he will lead them as surely as he had when Moses was alive. Nothing will make him abandon Israel.

4. **Courage supplied:** *"Be strong and courageous, because you will lead these people to inherit the land I swore to their ances-tors to give them. Be strong and very courageous"* *(vv. 6–7)*. Because God keeps his promises, Joshua can be strong and courageous. Hear the patience of a loving God who knows his man feels weak ("you will lead"), who knows that Joshua's only source of courage is his own trustworthy presence.

5. **Careful obedience:** *"Be careful to obey all the law my servant Moses gave you; do not turn from it to the right or to the left, that you may be successful wherever you go. Keep this Book of the Law always on your lips; meditate on it day and night, so that you may be careful to do everything written in it. Then you will be prosperous and successful"* (vv. 7–8). Here's the most daunting part. Joshua's leadership is first and foremost spiritual, and these people (like all humankind) have a history of disobedience to God's commands. They can try to muster perfect adherence to the law. They can meditate on God's word a lot and do all the things, and yet there's no way they will be "careful to do everything written in it." If their success depends on their obedience, they are doomed before they lace their sandals in the morning.

6. **Committed relationship:** *"Have I not commanded you? Be strong and courageous. Do not be afraid; do not be discouraged, for the LORD your God will be with you wherever you go"* (v. 9). Our God is just, righteous, and serious about obedience. But he also loves us beyond imagining. He knows our weakness better than we do, and he will never abandon us to it.

So how do these truths apply to the solo parent?

1. **Changed circumstances.** The single parent's situation in starkest terms: you are raising a child (or children) without the benefit of being married to the child's other parent. Together with our children, we will live a different life from two-parent families. Sounds obvious, but we might need to accept and mourn that our families don't look like we might have hoped or planned. That way we don't become discouraged by some mental picture of the family we don't have and we're freed to celebrate the one we do.

   Along these same lines, comparing our families to

two-parent families can lead to bitterness, pride, and envy (more on this later). Comparison will not help us be better parents, nor will it create healthy security for our kids.

2. **Unchanging grace.** God pours out grace on all families, whether the parents are married or not. That grace is by definition a gift, unearned and undeserved. We don't have to continue to apologize or feel guilty for sins confessed and repented. We don't have to be better than other moms and dads because there is only one of us. We will not receive less grace than two-parent families. His grace is sufficient for all of us (2 Cor. 12:9). That's a promise, and the one who promises is trustworthy and true.

3. **Steadfast presence.** Single parent, if you are a believer in Christ, you have his Spirit within you always. He will never leave you. He will never forsake you. He will never turn his back on you. You are sealed by the Holy Spirit. He will not abandon you, abuse you, die, become mentally ill, go to jail, succumb to addiction, or have an affair. Your family has his devoted and undivided attention, permanently. Nothing will ever separate you or your child from his love in Christ Jesus. His presence makes all the difference your family will ever need.

4. **Courage supplied.** As the leaders of our families, we need to be strong and courageous. The culture outside our homes and the sin within our hearts are enemies as scary as the warrior tribes Joshua faced. Our courage comes from knowing that God fights those battles for us and with us, just as he did for Israel.

I found this promise especially helpful with regard to spiritual leadership. My kids were wounded, and I worried that their dad's death might turn them against the God I wanted to teach them to trust. Joshua's task of leading Israel into the rest found in the promised land (Josh. 1:13) is a picture of the task we as parents have to lead our children into the Sabbath-rest of believing in Christ for their salvation (Heb. 4:10). Though he has a role, this responsibility is too big for Joshua, just like our children's salvation is too big for us. Our families need God, and what God is saying over and over is this: *we have him.*

Your children are in God's hands; their salvation belongs to him. The Holy Spirit does not need two parents to move through a family. Yes, the burdens of prayer, teaching, and discipleship fall on your shoulders, but you have within you the Spirit that raised Christ from the dead. Watch and see what the Lord can do in a family the world calls "broken."

5. **Careful obedience.** Married parents and single adults are just as sinful as single parents are. Mostly, single parents shoulder greater portions of loneliness, exhaustion, responsibility, and busyness (to name a few!) than married parents do, so we have to be careful not to justify giving in to certain temptations simply because we have certain hardships. But every last one of us, adults and children alike, needs to be justified by faith in Jesus. We obey because we love him, not because obedience will make our lives easier.

6. **Committed relationship.** As one writer put it, "God doesn't say, 'So, yeah, stick to those rules and you should be good.' . . . God instead promises Joshua [and us] relationship above all else. . . . God moves first—he comes down to Joshua because Joshua cannot meet him. God's promise in this passage [Joshua 1] points to his own fulfillment of the command. He answers his own requirements with a word of comfort."[1] God initiates his relationship with us, and God sustains his relationship with us. He gives us the strength and he gives us the courage. We don't have to work it up for ourselves, nor could we even if we tried.

Whatever lost or broken relationships may litter your land-scape, God's love for you is beyond human reckoning: "You asked for a loving God: you have one.... The consuming fire Himself, the Love that made the worlds, persistent as the artist's love for his work and despotic as a man's love for a dog, provident and venerable as a father's love for a child, jealous, inexorable, exacting as love between the sexes. How this should be, I do not know: it passes reason to explain why any creatures, not to say creatures such as we, should have a value so prodigious in their Creator's eyes."[2]

You and your children have prodigious value in God's eyes. His devotion to your family has broken the power of sin and death through the cross of Christ. Be strong and courageous. He is always with you.

My friend Cameron wrote this liturgy to use when he is fear-ful about whatever may lie ahead, and it encapsulates many of the truths we learn from Joshua:

> *I am not God. I cannot read the future. If I could, I am not capable of discerning if what's happening is good or bad.*
> *If it happens, it's within God's sovereign plan.*
> *If it happens, God will be there.*
> *If it happens, God will use it for his kingdom and greater glory.*
> *If it happens, God will be with me.*
> *If it happens, God will have a way forward for me.*
> *If it happens, God will use it to ultimately sanctify and bless me.*

What This Means for the Church

"You are so strong." "You are so wise." You've got nothing to be afraid of!" "You got this!"

Many kind, well-meaning people have said these things to me over my single-parent years. I appreciate the encouragement, I really do. But single parents don't need pep talks. We need Jesus.

For some single parents, "you got this" might feel something like chugging an energy drink. The vigor and confidence wear off. Sooner or later, we fail. That boost might last until the solo dad goes to pick up his daughter and ends up squabbling with his ex-wife in spite of his best intentions not to. The single mom might coast on the power of "you got this" until her work meeting runs long (again), she picks up her son from soccer late (again), and there's nothing in the fridge for dinner (again). "You got this" . . . until you don't.

For me, and others like me, pep talks about my strength only make me think of my weakness: the way I lose my temper, over-share with my teenager, neglect to pay a bill on time. Ironically, hearing "you're so strong" and "you got this!" make me ashamed and afraid to tell that well-meaning person how truly weak I am. When I hear those words, I feel burdened to keep up a facade of being strong. What I really need to hear is how Jesus is not ashamed of my weakness and wants to help me in it (Isa. 50:7).

Pep talks have no staying power because they aren't grounded in truth that has staying power. Rather than pretending Joshua has nothing to be afraid of, God encourages his new leader with truth about himself. God does not go all football coach on Joshua: "I have been training you for this moment all your life. You are a warrior! Now, go kill some gentiles!" God has prepped Joshua for this moment with years of learning under Moses, and Joshua's leadership is still a mixed bag of faith and failure, just like Moses's had been. God knows—and Joshua is humble enough to know— that Joshua will need a power far stronger than his own to carry out the tasks God will give him. That's why God's presence is essential to him, and to us.

So when you visit with a single-parent friend who needs to

talk about their worries and fears, your first job is to listen. Listen without judgment. Even if it sounds like whining to you—and sometimes it may be!—give them the gift of an uncritical ear. That person doesn't have a spouse to do this for them.

Second, don't try to fix it. If you're a parent, you know what it's like when childless people try to tell you how to raise kids. If you're a single person, you know what it's like to have married people try to tell you how to live your life. If you're not a single parent yourself, chances are you won't be able to offer solutions to many single-parent problems. Often people who are afraid won't be easily talked out of their fears. They need kind companionship more than they need answers or reasons they shouldn't feel the way they do.

If you do have ideas, offer them in humility. What matters most is not being right or feeling like you've helped. You are offering your friend a place to vent uncomfortable emotions, and it's going to be hard to resist hurrying to make them feel better or dismissing their feelings because you think they are wrong for feeling the way they do. Offer your presence and your prayers as you listen, simply hoping your single-parent friend feels understood.

Finally, when you glimpse an opportunity, praise the mom or dad who may never hear, "Well done." One single mom shared the story of her daughter's tantrum at the playground. When she finally calmed her angry child and sent her off to play, she was embarrassed to turn back to her friend, who had witnessed the whole meltdown. Instead, her friend said, "Wow. You're a really good mom." Without a husband to be a sounding board, this single mom questioned her parenting constantly, and no one ever told her she was doing a good job raising her child. She needed to hear it.

Above all else, give your single-parent friends the gift of encouragement that is stable, reliable, and eternal. Give them the comfort that is truly comfort. Give them the gospel.

We are all weak and sinful, and our best intentions are no more dependable than the weather. No matter how much parents want to love their children well, our sin and shortsightedness mean that our efforts will always fall short. But because of Jesus, that's okay. God doesn't expect us to be what we are not. Through the sinless life of Jesus, his willing death on the cross, his glorious resurrection, and the gift of the Spirit's indwelling, we will never be alone or helpless, even as we flail in utter inadequacy. And when we do sin, disappoint, and make mistakes, our God is a redeeming God. Whether we're single or married, our children's thriving—and our own—isn't our responsibility to carry.

Single parents need exactly the kind of encouragement you need: the hope of the gospel, the truth of his Word, and the love of a friend.

Maria's Ebenezer Stones

Single mom Maria tells of stepping out to get the mail just before dinner one night. She was feeling pretty good about things: dinner was in the oven, homework was underway, and the kids were getting along. But sitting in the mailbox was a nastygram from her ex-husband's lawyer. Instantly her peace of mind pitched into a mental dumpster fire. Years of fear that she might lose her children to a man she did not trust came rushing back to torment her.

Sitting at the dinner table with her children, forcing herself to eat and make conversation while fear howled in her head, Maria remembered how faithful God had been to her family. She silently rehearsed all the times God had made a way when there seemed to be no way. By the end of the meal, she was calm and even content enough to focus on being with her kids. Though she faced a new legal battle that would last for several months, she found some rest from her fears in God's track record of goodness, and in time the latest crisis was resolved.

As she was telling me this story, I remembered the prophet Samuel's Ebenezer stone, a memorial he set up to help the Israelites remember a victory over the enemy Philistines, saying, "Thus far the LORD has helped us" (1 Sam. 7:12). As testimonies to God's faithfulness in our personal stories, "Ebenezers" are vital markers in the life of any Christian. Sometimes when I am discouraged, I need help to remember them. I imagine you do too. If you and I are close enough, if we know each other's fears—and each other's Ebenezers—we can remind each other of the ways Jesus has been our steadfast Savior.

My brother, my sister, this is something we can do for each other.

four

God's Comfort in Our Grief

This is why I weep
    and my eyes overflow with tears.
No one is near to comfort me,
    no one to restore my spirit.
My children are destitute
    because the enemy has prevailed. (Lamentations 1:16)

The Lord is close to the brokenhearted
    and saves those who are crushed in spirit. (Psalm 34:18)

Anthony hardly remembers the first few months after his young wife died of cancer, but he does remember the guilt.

Two of his wife's friends handled logistics around the home, and two others cleaned the house and folded laundry weekly. His Sunday school class handled meals (for how long, he doesn't exactly recall—months? A year? A long time, he is certain). Anthony went to work, came home, and, through the brain fog of grief, tried to focus on his small children every evening. At ages three, six, and eight, they cried for their mother often, especially the older two. They asked him questions about her death, and he stared at them mutely; he felt strangely unmoved by their tears.

He worried that his numbness was sin. He only wanted to crawl into bed and wait for sleep to relieve the overwhelming guilt he felt for not being able to comfort his children.

Writer Clarissa Moll was widowed when her husband, Rob, died in a hiking accident, leaving her with four children. She tells of holding her son as he sobbed:

> No more powerless feeling exists in all the world than to see your child endure a pain you cannot take away, you cannot assuage even a bit. There exists no distraction, no encouragement, no reward, no gift, no friendship that can fill the aching void that compels him to tears. Death has pierced his tender life and sorrow now has darkened every part. Behind every smile he hides a broken heart.[1]

A grieving single parent cannot crawl into bed and hide. They have to get up every day, make breakfast, drive the carpool, and go to work, all while continuing to care for children who are often wrestling with their own grief. In the midst of sorrow, the single parent must have both the ministry of the Holy Spirit and the care of their church to sustain them in their loss.

The Grief-Stricken Parent

As I mentioned earlier, single parents often describe the loss of a spouse as an amputation. Listen to Dr. Jaimie Shores of Johns Hopkins describe amputation, and think of it in terms of divorce or death: "The loss or removal of a body part [spouse] . . . can be a life changing experience affecting your ability to move, work, interact with others and maintain your independence. Continuing pain, phantom limb phenomena and emotional trauma can complicate recovery."[2] Amputations occur because of sudden trauma, such as an accident or a chronic disease that threatens the health of the whole body. Limbs that were missing at birth can be called a congenital amputation.

The analogy is an apt one. In the mysterious intimacy of marriage, husband and wife become "one flesh" before God and humanity. Husbands are called to love their wives "as their own bodies. . . . After all, no one ever hated their own body, but they feed and care for their body, just as Christ does the church—for we are members of his body. 'For this reason a man will leave his father and mother and be united to his wife, and the two will become one flesh'" (Eph. 5:28–31). The union is physical (husband and wife share bodies), emotional (love, not hate), practical (they establish a new home together), and above all spiritual: "This is a profound mystery—but I am talking about Christ and the church" (v. 32).

To lose one's spouse is to lose a piece of oneself. It's no wonder that a ruptured marriage is so profoundly painful, affecting not only parents but also their children physically, emotionally, practically, and spiritually. Perhaps the marriage crumbled, dissolving between parents who felt powerless to preserve their union; maybe it imploded, detonated by infidelity, addiction, or violence. Sometimes a partner dies or deserts, or never commits at all. Whether the end is sudden and shocking or a long, slow torture, parents and children are left to grieve.

Grieving Parents Caring for Grieving Children

In the months after my husband died, I operated in triage mode. Whichever child was struggling most openly got the bulk of my attention. I knew even then that just because the other two weren't visibly upset, that did not mean they were not also gripped with sadness or anger. They simply weren't expressing it. I felt powerless to help the crying child and even more powerless to help the silent sufferer. There was less of me to go around—literally less of me because part of me was gone—and I too was hobbling through each day, aching with the absence of my phantom-limb husband, just as they were gutted by the absence of their father.

I suspect that Anthony (from the previous story) wasn't sinning when he failed to comfort his children. He was learning to live with the amputation, and it would take some time before he would once again move through the world with ease.

Barnabas Piper describes a similar powerlessness to bear his daughters' grief when he and their mother divorced:

> You can't go in and tell them everything's gonna be okay. You can only apologize so many times, and you can't cast blame on the other parent . . . you can't be divisive. So you end up just absorbing a lot of their pain, a lot of their tears, a lot of their questions that you can't answer, either because you don't know the answer or because it's just not helpful to give the answer. There's an enormous amount of just swallowing the pain of your kids and taking those blows on your back. It's a lot worse than hurting yourself. . . . As a parent, you're responsible for your kids, but you can't fix your kids and you can't fix their situations and you can't remove their burdens. I would have taken it all if I could have, but they had to go to school, they had to navigate this [divorce] with friends, they had to move from having one home to having two homes, and all of these changes are a loss for them. It's way worse when they hurt, than when I hurt, always.[3]

Parents who have always been single also grieve their inability to spare their children the pain of an absent parent. I recently talked with a single mom after a panel I participated in on single motherhood. Through tears she spoke of sitting with her adopted teenaged sons in the pews at church, mourning all that they would miss because they were growing up without a father. During the week, the absence of male presence did not feel so acute, but with dads all around them on Sunday mornings, she couldn't help but grieve the father her boys would never have.

Children who are born into a one-parent home are born into a loss, and growing up becomes a process of discovering that loss. In her memoir *Finding My Father: How the Gospel Heals the Pain of Fatherlessness*, spoken word artist Blair Linne details her gradual awakening to all she missed out on without her father in the home: "We see the effects of not having our dad—the gash, the tears, the steady dribble of heartache inside of us; the slow, creeping onset of pain and grief as the breach of relationship begins to boil over into different areas of our life. But what most of us never do is work our way back to the original cause."[4] Grief snuck up on her as she realized all she had missed out on because of her dad's absence: provision, protection, attention, affection, and security were all stretched thin or absent in her home. She had a loving and capable mom, but the lack of a stable marriage and the God-ordained "covering"[5] of her father left her vulnerable and afraid.

By God's grace, Linne was able to express her anger and sadness to her father. He responded with vulnerability, sharing that he had never known what it was like to have his dad at home either. His openness brought a measure of healing and redemption: "He let me see his frailty that day, and it's something that has cuddled my story like a weighted blanket." Many other kids will never have the opportunity to speak openly to the parent who has hurt them, or they may not be willing to risk the relationship they do have by expressing their grief. Likewise, a grieving parent struggles to care for the child who is grieving but unable or unwilling to put words to it. The temptation for an exhausted parent is to decide that child is okay and move on.

Three Caveats about Grieving Children

First, mourning a deep loss happens over a lifetime. Parent and child are forever changed. Please hear me say this: we have a God who redeemed the unjust death of his only, perfect, sinless Son. If he can redeem the murder of Jesus and use it for his glory and for our good, then he can absolutely redeem whatever losses your family has suffered. Neither you nor your child has to live a less-than life because they are being raised by one parent. Yes, you will have challenges. That does not mean life cannot be rich, fruitful, and fulfilling. Even if someone tries to misuse the verse as a bandage for your amputation, Romans 8:28 is *true*: "We know that in all things God works for the good of those who love him, who have been called according to his purpose." The divorce, desertion, or death was not good, but the God who is able to raise Jesus—and us!—from the dead is able to produce perseverance, character, and hope from whatever has happened in your life and in your child's (see Rom. 5:1–5). Fight to keep your eyes on the cross, and show the cross to your kids every chance you get.

Second, children who have suffered loss will likely process it differently than adults. Younger children often experience grief as sudden, violent emotional storms: they are overcome, the tears or anger (or both) seem to explode out of them, and then the storm passes and they run off to play Legos. Teenagers might brood, getting stuck in their sadness; they might pretend they are fine; they might act out in uncharacteristic ways. Regardless of their age, most kids are reactive. Because they need to feel safe, they tune in to their parent's emotional wavelength and respond either by matching their parent's grief or by expressing its opposite. In the case of divorce, the child might even feel one way with one parent and another way with the other. You cannot erase or fix their pain, but you can show them how to lament and carry it to the Father in prayer. You can reassure them that God's family will bear the burden of grief with them (Gal. 6:2).

Finally, be aware that grief will recede and reappear throughout the child's life. This happens for adults too, but it's even truer for children whose connection with their parent has been lost or broken. Passing through milestones—graduations, first jobs, weddings, and especially the births of their own children—can trigger profound sadness, anger, depression, or anxiety. As a parent, you don't have to fear these moments or be caught off guard. Prepare for transitions in your kids' lives through prayer, and stand ready to comfort and advise them if they need you. If it's possible, an established relationship with a trusted church friend, mentor, or counselor can be a huge gift to your child. It doesn't always have to be you. Often our kids want to protect us and avoid any conversations that might dredge up our own grief or shame. That's okay. That's one of the reasons God gave us his church.

The God of All Comfort

God has ordained that our comfort come in relationship with him and in community with his church:

> Praise be to the God and Father of our Lord Jesus Christ, the Father of compassion and the God of all comfort, who comforts us in all our troubles, so that we can comfort those in any trouble with the comfort we ourselves receive from God. For just as we share abundantly in the sufferings of Christ, so also our comfort abounds through Christ. If we are distressed, it is for your comfort and salvation; if we are comforted, it is for your comfort, which produces in you patient endurance of the same sufferings we suffer. And our hope for you is firm, because we know that just as you share in our sufferings, so also you share in our comfort. (2 Cor. 1:3–7)

Here Paul shares a number of valuable insights about how members of God's family give and receive comfort from God and each other.

God is the *Father of compassion*, meaning that compassion is his very nature. All compassion starts with him and flows from him to us, often through other people. Remembering that compassion is *who he is* relieves our fears that God is distant or stern or mad at us.

All comfort that is truly comfort comes from God. Anything else in which we look for comfort will ultimately not sustain us. As wonderful as the good pleasures of this world can be—like a bowl of chocolate ice cream, a snuggle with a freshly bathed, sleepy toddler, a home-cooked dinner with close friends, or an invigorating morning run—they are temporary. Our comfort lies in the unchanging love of God and his total commitment to our good, and our evidence lies in the cross and the resurrection. "Heaven and earth will pass away," but God's promises to us never will (Matt. 24:35). No one is more reliably loving than God. He will never leave (Heb. 13:5), hold a grudge (Ps. 103:9), or die. He has already died for you. Now he lives to intercede for you and your children (Heb. 7:25). Could anything be more comforting than that?

God comforts us in *all our troubles*. He does not distinguish between the troubles other people have caused us, the troubles we have brought on ourselves, and the troubles that come from living in a fallen world. (Remember, he's the Father of compassion.)

The comfort we receive is more than enough for our own wounds, and so we have comfort to spare for *those in any trouble*. Comfort multiplies as we share it! Our comfort *abounds through Christ*: the joy, hope, peace, and love we feel when we focus our minds on the work of Christ and press it into our hearts (especially through worship, service, and the reading of Scripture) are a fountain of living water that will never run dry. Jesus himself is the "consolation of Israel" (Luke 2:25).

In God's marvelous economy, our suffering is not wasted. Our distress takes on dignity and even purpose when God uses it as a means to comfort and save. To be clear, God does not afflict us with suffering so he can work through us to help other people. Suffering results from living in a fallen world damaged by sin. But this is how Romans 8:28 works: God can use even the deepest pain for his redemptive purposes.

What This Means for the Church

One of the hallmarks of deep grief is loneliness (which we'll talk more about in chapter 6). Loss isolates us, especially the loss of a spouse or a parent. These relationships are one of a kind, irreplaceable, never to be repeated. Instinctively we know that nothing we say or do could ever change that fact for our grieving friend. But if we keep our distance from the grieving one, we only add to their loss.

I've mentioned how my husband's death dropped my sons and me into a parallel universe. We could never cross back over into the life that was, nor did it seem that our friends, even our closest ones, could go to that new universe with us. *Their* closest relationships were intact. *Their* family was the same. *Their* future still looked as it had before. It felt like a gulf had opened wide between us and the people we needed most, and it seemed that gap could never be bridged.

God intends members of his church to share in their varied sufferings, but this sharing is complicated for both the grieving and the comforter. Clarissa Moll speaks openly about how disorienting it felt to go to church as a grieving widow and mother:

The church has always felt like a second home to me, so it was strange, after my husband died, to feel like I didn't belong anymore. A lot of church's programming is designed for families, and we were a strange-looking family now. As a mom with four kids, we just didn't fit anywhere. I didn't fit in couples' Sunday school classes anymore, and just the structure [of the church] . . . didn't take into account the fact that my family looked different now, and that I carried [grief] that was really heavy. . . . Church services generally spend very little time in lament . . . so for people who are sitting utterly broken in the pews, it can easily feel like the church just isn't for them anymore.[6]

The passage from 2 Corinthians 1:3–7 is the bridge we need to reach each other when loss separates us.

Crossing that bridge can feel super awkward. When he declared, ". . . the Lord comforts us, not to make us comfortable, but to make us comforters," Baptist pastor John Henry Jowett was talking about 2 Corinthians 1.[7] It's easy to think you have nothing to offer your single-parent friend. If you're happily married, what could you possibly say to your friend whose wife left him for another man? If your husband coaches your daughter's soccer team and pays the bills on time, what could you possibly say to the woman whose ex skips town to avoid visitation and child support payments? You will keep your distance if you think you have to solve your friend's problems or say just the right thing to make them stop hurting. You were not called to fix anything for anyone else. Let's face it, you can't even fix your own problems. You were, however, called to love. Rest assured, if you don't try to love and care for that friend, you will only compound their pain and reinforce their isolation. To see what this love does (and does not) look like, let's turn to the book of Job before we cross our 2 Corinthians bridge.

How the Church Can Share the Suffering: Presence

As the saying goes, Job's comforters did well until they opened their mouths.

To be fair, Job's comforters have become a punch line, but their original instincts were sound. As soon as they heard of Job's catastrophe, Eliphaz, Bildad, and Zophar "set out from their homes and met together by agreement to go and sympathize with him and comfort him" (Job 2:11). Job's grief had rendered him unrecognizable (a tender reminder of how profound loss can make the suffering one feel alienated even from himself). But rather than stay away, repelled by the change in Job or frightened by the depth of his suffering, "they began to weep aloud, and they tore their robes and sprinkled dust on their heads" (v. 12). Their commitment to suffer with him endured, as they sat with Job on the ground for seven days and seven nights in speechless respect for his pain: "No one said a word to him, because they saw how great his suffering was" (v. 13).

Clarissa Moll saw this kind of love in powerful action. Their family had moved to the East Coast only a year before her husband died, so she decided to have his funeral at their original home church back in the Pacific Northwest. Standing in the narthex before her husband's memorial service, Moll was stunned to see a familiar face coming toward her:

> It is my kids' youth pastor, who has flown 3,000 miles to be at this memorial service. I had no idea that she would be arriving. We'd known her for only a year because we were new at the church. That statement of commitment to my family was so powerful. . . . That's what we need to do. We don't need more parachurch ministries, we don't need a better meal train, or a handyman service. We need the gift of presence. The amazing thing is, that's something anyone can do. You don't have to be on pastoral staff, you don't have to be a lay leader. All you have to do is commit to showing up.[8]

I'll reiterate Moll's words: *anyone can show up.* In my interviews with single parents, I often heard that pastors and elders do a better job with offering presence and comfort than regular church members do. I share this not as criticism but as a reminder that every Christian has the Holy Spirit within, every Christian has at least some experience of suffering, and every Christian has access to God's Word, which teaches us what God's comfort looks like and how to offer it. Yes, pastors and elders often have training in grief support, but like anyone, church leaders learned to offer care the hard way: by showing up. Any brother or sister in the body of Christ can do that—imperfectly, but with genuine love.

Single-parent families need your presence. They need you to come close and stay close. They know you feel awkward, which makes your willingness to swallow the weirdness and stay close even more meaningful. If you aren't afraid of their grief or anger or despair, your courage encourages them. In times of intense sorrow, the Spirit may lead you into silence, even when you want so badly to fill the space with words. Sometimes there are no words. Certainly nothing you can say will fix the sadness of an abandoned wife or a child whose parent never shows up. If you have a lot of words, pour them out silently in prayer. God is certainly listening, and he will sustain you in your discomfort even as he is sustaining your hurting friend. Their Helper is also your Helper. Your commitment to be faithful honors him. You don't have to do it perfectly. Just show up and pray. Listen to the Spirit and listen to your friend.

How the Church Can Share the Suffering: Words of Comfort

Job's friends get in trouble because they don't offer Job the truth about who God is. Their theology stinks: they blame Job, they blame God, and they show a remarkable lack of that compassion that God is the Father of.

Our passage from 2 Corinthians 1:3–7 instructs us in how to help our grieving brothers and sisters. We don't offer a sentimental compassion laced with platitudes, half-truths, and falsehood: "God never gives us more than we can handle." "I believe God will bring you a new wife, and can I set you up with ___?" "He's in a better place." None of that will hold up to the whole counsel of Scripture.

True comfort originates with the God of all comfort. This means speaking the truth about him to your grieving friend. You don't have to know exactly how someone feels to offer them the consolation you have found in the Lord in your own trials. Yes, we each find a certain fellowship with others who have walked the same roads. If you are living with a chronic illness, you will not only find solace in commiseration with others who share your illness, you'll also find practical ideas about how to live well in your circumstance. The same is certainly true for single parents. But what it's like to be a single parent should never prevent you from offering the comfort of the gospel and the reassurance of God's enduring kindness. The hope of any Christian undergoing trial lies in the character of God himself.

Take care not to offer the truths of Scripture as if they are platitudes. Even as you speak truth about God to your hurting friend, be sensitive to the moment. Say, for instance, your single-mom friend is enraged by Instagram posts showing her ex-husband's new wife cuddling *your friend's children*, who are wearing expensive Christmas outfits your friend could never afford to buy for them. Now is not the time to remind your friend that she is the apple of God's eye (which she is) or that God is meeting all their needs (true, just not helpful here). Her anger may sound like bitterness and complaining to you, and it might be. Don't judge her—in the same circumstances you might be more bitter than she is—but in humility and patience "restore [her] in a spirit of gentleness" (Gal. 6:1 ESV). Remind her that God hears her cries, that he is close to the brokenhearted, that she can tell him anything she is thinking and feeling. In moments of intense hurt, she doesn't need to count her blessings, she needs to lament. Biblical lament will lead her back to the character of God, the *Father of compassion* and the *God of all comfort*. His goodness will restore her to gratitude and contentment, even if it takes a long time.

Partners in Suffering, Partners in Comfort

Let's drill down into 2 Corinthians 1:7, which reads, "Our hope for you [our confident expectation of good for you] is firmly grounded [assured and unshaken], since we know that just as you share *as partners* in our sufferings, so also you share *as partners* in our comfort" (AMP).

By showing you how very different single-parent family life can be, I never want to imply that single parents are shipwrecked on Single-Parent Island (though it can feel that way some days) and that those who don't live there can't expect to understand or offer consolation. If that were true, then Paul's words here couldn't be. Paul writes to the Corinthians, who do not share his unique mission to be an apostle, a missionary, and one of the divinely inspired authors of the Holy Scriptures. Few people in history have borne as much responsibility as Paul, and none of them could have known exactly what it felt like to be him. But because they love him, their hearts are bound up with his. When he hurts, they hurt; when he receives comfort, they receive comfort (Rom. 12:15).

We have an obligation and a duty to empathize with our brothers and sisters, but even more, we have the *privilege* of suffering with them. As U2 sings, "We *get to* carry each other."[9] Job's comforters sprinkled dirt on their own heads; they sat on the ground and wept as their way of saying, "We will go with you through it all. We will not leave you to bear this alone."

And though their words of comfort are miserable, Job's friends have a front-row seat to Job's new understanding of who God is. We cannot say for sure if they were able to hear God speaking to Job, but afterward God turns directly to Eliphaz, rebukes him for not speaking truthfully about God's character, and through Job's prayer offers the friends mercy and grace, not dealing with them "according to [their] folly" (Job 42:8). Their intimate proximity to their suffering friend will correct their false view of God and allow them to worship him in truth instead of foolishness. Because they share Job's mourning, they share his comfort.

Sharing suffering is a two-way street. The single parent must lay down their defenses and allow trustworthy people to come close enough to know their grief. For families who have experienced loss, abandonment, or abuse, vulnerability is a kind of suffering in itself. They will feel safest with Christians who are truly humble, who don't have all the answers but are willing to *suffer with*, whatever that means, for as long as it takes.

— five —

God's Strength in Our Exhaustion

Come to me, all you who are weary and burdened, and I will give you rest. Take my yoke upon you and learn from me, for I am gentle and humble in heart, and you will find rest for your souls. For my yoke is easy and my burden is light. (Matthew 11:28–30)

Willie tells me that the moment the delivery nurse placed her newborn son in her arms, she knew her husband would leave her.

Born with a cleft palate, health issues, and learning disabilities, Willie's adult son now holds a full-time job making deliveries. Alongside his older sisters and his mom, he learned to love Jesus in a local church. By the grace of God, he is thriving as a young man making his way in the world and hopes to move out on his own someday.

Every step of the way, Willie fought for him. Without any support from her ex-husband, Willie nursed him through numerous expensive surgeries. She petitioned his school repeatedly for special services, which he was denied for years despite his teachers' agreement that he qualified. She did this all while working full time and raising her daughters too.

Her son faced a lot of challenges, and Willie has been glad to tackle every obstacle in his way. But she did it all alone, far more alone than she needed to be. She felt continually responsible to educate her church because they did not seem to understand how to help her bear the burdens of poverty, divorce, and caring for a child with special needs. The church assigned a supportive elder to stay in close touch with Willie. But while her children were growing up, their family did not develop real fellowship with other families. Though they were always welcome at church events, no one ever invited Willie and her kids into their home to grill out or watch the Super Bowl.

All those years of fighting for her child alone made Willie very, very tired.

Here's a riff off the opening line of Jane Austen's *Pride and Prejudice*: it is a truth, universally acknowledged, that a single parent in possession of one or more children, must be in want of a nap.

At least a nap. A season of hibernation might be more like it.

As I interviewed single parents for this book, the chronic busyness, the unshared weight of raising a child, and the resulting exhaustion were almost always the first thing a parent would mention. "How are you?" I would ask, and the answer was nearly always "tired," sometimes "exhausted," paired with "busy."

To be fair, *all* parents are tired and busy. From the time we arrive home from the hospital with that precious bundle, our sleep is less important than the urgently expressed needs and wants of the helpless little one in our care. It's exhausting, but it's part of the parenting gig, and it's certainly easier when the other parent takes over so you can occasionally sleep in.

But the single parent doesn't have anyone else to get up with the sun every single day. The single parent plans for every dinner and has to remember every oil change. Nor is there anyone else to fetch the middle-of-the-night cup of water, to find the thermometer in the dark without waking anyone else, or to silence the beeping smoke detector because you forgot to change the batteries again (and because those batteries never die at 1:00 p.m., only at 1:00 a.m.). No one is coming to help. If an urgent need is going to be met, they have to be the one to meet it, even if cleaning up vomit makes them vomit. Just knowing that makes the exhaustion oppressive.

The Twenty-Four-Hour Parent

If parenting were a hurdle race (and don't some days feel that way?), married parents are running a relay. Single parents never get to pass the baton, unless they co-parent, and then the handoff can be tricky indeed. In two-parent families, there's at least the possibility of some job sharing at home. As a single parent, you might not even get to share being on call; as a co-parent, you might share being on call with someone you don't feel you can trust. If your child needs something, tag, you're it.

Say you receive a call from school or daycare. Your child is sick. You leave work to pick up the child. You need to get back to work because your job is how you pay for the medicine, but there's no one to stay with the sick child. When you do get back to work, the pressure to produce and perform only intensifies when you lead a one-paycheck family.

Then there's the stress of round-the-clock accessibility: as a single parent, you feel you cannot turn off your phone. Any random notification could be from your child, or the school, or the police . . . Maybe you don't want to turn off your texts because your daughter is staying at her dad's tonight and she might need to vent about her lack of a prom date. Maybe you're at work in the wee hours of the evening, hoping your child doesn't wake from a nightmare with only a babysitter to comfort him. Heaven forbid that you be unavailable, especially to your children, especially if you are their only parent. Getting off the grid, even for a few hours, does not feel like an option.

All of this means that the mental toll of being a solo parent is sometimes higher than the physical burden. The single parent schedules every dentist appointment, signs every permission slip, buys every pair of cleats, and makes every late-night run for posterboard—or has to coordinate these details with the other parent. They have to decide where the child will go to school, what the curfew will be, and who their teenager can hang out with. The single parent has to remember every rule and enforce them all, with consideration for both fairness among siblings and the needs of each particular child. There's no one else to teach the teenager to drive—a uniquely terrifying experience—or to attend the possibly miserable parent-teacher conference. Children have to be fed, bathed, and clothed and trained to brush their teeth, clean their rooms, and use a knife. And as one single mom said, figuring out by yourself how to discipline *and* retain a warm emotional connection at the same time feels pretty much impossible. All responsibilities rest on one person who is not going to get a break until the child grows up and moves away (which is yet another hurdle to face alone).

The emotional toll might be the highest of all. All the fears, worries, and middle-of-the-night-freakouts fall on one pair of tense and lonely shoulders, and there's no one to offer a back rub. We worry we are failing our children. We worry about what we might be failing to worry about because there isn't another set of eyes to see how our child might be struggling. You have lost (if you ever had) your intimate connection with the other person who might love your child as much as you do. Even if that person is still in your child's life, he or she has become distant and alien. Unlike a married parent, you may not feel you can rely on their love for the child you share, or on your ability to communicate well with that other parent.

All parents bear burdens for their children, but the single parent bears them alone.

There's no soft place to land, no way to take our hands off the steering wheel and let someone else drive. The single parent functions like the backstop at the baseball field: nothing can get by them, or chaos takes over. Unlike the backstop, however, people aren't made of concrete and steel. Being tall and wide and strong enough to stop every stray ball at any moment is not sustainable.

Jesus Invites the Single Parent to Share His Yoke

Come to me, all you who are weary and burdened, and I will give you rest. Take my yoke upon you and learn from me, for I am gentle and humble in heart, and you will find rest for your souls. For my yoke is easy and my burden is light. (Matt. 11:28–32)

This passage has been in memes, printed on mugs and T-shirts, cross-stitched on pillows, and tossed out as a platitude far too often. Don't let familiarity rob these words of their power, but meditate on them slowly. Which words ring out in your soul when you read them today?

"*Come to me . . .*" Jesus extends an openhearted invitation, not only to follow him, as he has done earlier in Matthew (4:19), but to come *to* him. It's personal. It's almost as if he's holding out his hand and smiling, looking you in the eye with compassion and delight. There's nothing begrudging here, nothing but warmth in these words. Coming to Jesus is like walking into outstretched arms.

"*. . . all you who are weary and burdened.*" Jesus does not discriminate based on why you are tired or why your burdens are heavy. No matter if your troubles are largely of your own making, the result of someone else's hard heart or bad choices, or (most likely) some combination of the two, Jesus wants you, burdens and all. He wants your family and your children, even with your past, even with your pain. No hint of rejection, scrutiny, or judgment here. He holds back nothing from you.

"*I will give you rest.*" Do you remember what it is to rest? Do you wonder what that might look like in your single-parent life? With kids and work and everything you have to take care of, rest sounds like a miracle on par with the parting of the Red Sea. You wonder how Jesus helps with the never-ending list of things to do, not to mention the things that never get done. And yet he promises rest, and God cannot lie. He wants to give you a gift if you will but come receive it by faith.

"*Take my yoke upon you and learn from me . . .*" The infinite difference between our strength and Jesus's strength means he will be pulling the load. Sharing the yoke keeps us close to Jesus and teaches us to move with him. Everything is much, much harder than it needs to be when we strain against the yoke by trying to go our own way or by trying to pull as if it all depends on us.

"*. . . for I am gentle and humble in heart.*" The gentleness of Jesus comforts those whom life has treated harshly. Trusting his gentleness brings rest when we are short on cash, in a power struggle with an ex, or lying awake worrying about a depressed child.

"*And you will find rest for your souls.*" Jesus reiterates the promise of rest. He really means it. Maybe it feels like God failed to keep a promise when your marriage fell apart or your spouse died or your boyfriend left. Pour out your feelings of loss and even betrayal, if you feel God has let you down. Job felt that way, and Jeremiah, and David. Even Jesus raised the anguished question, "My God, my God, why have you forsaken me?" (Matt. 27:46). Biblical lament unburdens our souls by leading us to confront the sovereignty and, eventually, the goodness of God. Jesus does not offer a rest that gets us out from under our responsibilities, but rather soul rest, which is the peace that passes understanding even smack in the middle of your exhausting single-parent life. Rest for our souls flows from the cross, where Jesus dealt once and for all with our sin. That cross shows us the price Jesus was willing to pay to reconcile us to himself. In Christ we are children of a compassionate Father who knows what we need and gives it freely. We cannot fathom how deeply he loves us.

So the rest he gives is not passive, as if Jesus were inviting us to snooze in a hammock (though that kind of rest is certainly needed and even holy). In these verses from Matthew, Jesus echoes Jeremiah 6:16, which reads,

> Stand at the crossroads and look;
> ask for the ancient paths,
> ask where the good way is, and walk in it,
> and you will find rest for your souls.

Our rest in Jesus involves actively examining our lives and asking God to show us the way he has for us, and then obeying his voice. We rest from anxiety, worry, fear, and stress by trusting that he will lead—"This is the way; walk in it" (Isa. 30:21)—and that walking in his ways will bring us peace (Prov. 3:5–6). We don't have to figure it all out by ourselves. Peace does not come from God removing our problems but from his presence in the middle of those problems. He walks with us, side by side.

"*My yoke is easy and my burden is light.*" The yoke of Jesus is "easy" in the sense that it requires us to prove nothing. God looks at us and sees his Son, who has already lived the sinless life we couldn't live and died the death we deserved. Jesus secured our righteousness, so we don't have to (we can't), and our children don't have to secure it for us either. With that pressure relieved, we can carry the pressures of our daily lives in constant connection with our infinitely strong yokemate, Jesus. Moving under his light yoke doesn't remove all our cares, but it does make the burden of them lighter. With greater trust comes a measure of relief.

We can also ask other people for help when we need it because we no longer have to justify ourselves by meeting every single need in our own strength, giving our children everything they want (or everything their friends have), or raising kids whose outward behavior appears to validate our parenting.

Our children are not burdens; they are gifts and blessings. But sometimes, in our extreme weakness and exhaustion, in our fear of failing them and the sincere desire to love them well, we experience them as burdens. The fear of failing them can be so overwhelming that it causes some parents to flee because they know instinctively that their weakness is too great.

Single parent, if you have distanced yourself from your child in some way, or even failed to show up at all, come to Jesus. If you have found your child to be a burden instead of God's blessing, you aren't the only parent who has ever felt this way. Jesus holds out his hand to you and invites you to come to him. He invites you to repent of your distance from your child. Return to him. Ask him to restore the relationship and heal any guilt you may have. Ask for his forgiveness; you've got it.

Children become burdens when we think we have to meet all their needs in our own human strength, but Jesus bears the burden for your child's life. Trusting him with your child can lift your sense of exhaustion and free you to better love your child. Yoked and strong and by your side, Jesus will teach you how to carry your child in *his* strength. Let our heavenly Father parent you as you learn to parent your child.

What This Means for the Church

Two episodes from the life of Moses offer insight into how members of Christ's church can come alongside single parents and bear their burdens with them (Gal. 6:2), both spiritually and practically.

Let's consider what an enormous task God gives Moses. He leads a nation of up to two million Israelites out of slavery in Egypt into the wilderness. They look to him for everything: food, water, protection, wisdom, and spiritual guidance. He is general and diplomat, leader and decision-maker, judge and conscience, provider and protector for the entire nation. Above all, he is the mediator between God and his chosen people, who are characterized by a spirit of complaint, a bent toward idolatry, and a tendency to be uncooperative (much like kids at times). To complicate matters, Israel is trespassing on enemy territory on their way to the promised land.

None of us lead a family as large as his, but Moses functioned like a single parent to the entire nation of Israel.

In our first episode, the Amalekites attack (Exodus 17). While Joshua leads the troops in battle, Moses commits to standing on a hillside above the battle with his hands raised in intercessory prayer. As long as Moses's hands remain raised, the Israelites control the battle, but whenever his hands come down, the tide turns in favor of the Amalekites. But God does not send Moses to that hillside alone. Aaron and Hur stand with him and attend to his needs even as he prays. When Moses's legs get tired, they pull up a stone so the old man can sit; when his arms grow tired, "Aaron and Hur [hold] his hands up—one on one side, one on the other—so that his hands [remain] steady till sunset" (Ex. 17:12).

What a stunningly simple and profound picture of how we can sustain each other in prayer. Above the battle the scene is tender and intimate, with Aaron and Hur literally holding Moses in his physical weakness, yet God's power is unleashed in the brutal conflict below. Victory comes as God is honored by their united persistence in prayer. The Holy Spirit groans within us when we don't have words (Rom. 8:26), but we are also sustained through the prayers of other people, prayers that hold our hands up to God in yearning need when we cannot find the words or the strength in ourselves.

God intends his children to contend for one another in prayer. Pray for the single-parent families among you. Ask how you can hold up holy hands on their behalf; know the battles they are facing so that you can stand with them; ask them to pray for you too. They will be strengthened by your willingness to come close in prayer, steadied as you remain close to see God bring them through the fight. God will give you a bird's-eye view of his goodness in their trials, and you will have gained a brother or sister who can stand with you in yours.

God not only provides spiritual support for Moses, he has an eye to the practical too, and in the second episode, we see that God doesn't expect Moses to do it all. God's children should never be without hands-on help. Moses will learn to prioritize, delegate, and ask for help.

Moses's father-in-law Jethro comes to visit and points out that Moses can share some of the leadership. Because he is the only judge over the people, from dawn till dusk, Moses hears the disputes of the people. Jethro is flabbergasted: "What you are doing is not good. You and these people who come to you will only wear yourselves out. The work is too heavy for you; you cannot handle it alone" (Ex. 18:17–18). Acknowledging that yes, it's Moses's job to "be the people's representative before God," to teach and to "show them the way they are to live and how they are to behave" (vv. 19–20), Jethro urges him to train other leaders to take on some of the responsibilities. He promises that if Moses does so, he will "be able to stand the strain, and all these people will go home satisfied" (v. 23).

Church, we cannot take the job of parent from a weary single mom or dad—nor would they want us to—but we can be co-laborers, bearing the work not only of prayer but also of carpooling, home maintenance, or help with math homework. Your single-parent friend is racing to clear the hurdles alone. Offer to take the baton wherever you are able so they can sit and rest a spell. There's only so much you can do, but then again, the body of Christ can do so much to help the single parent and their child.

Let's Get Practical

The following quote has been attributed to Teresa of Ávila: "Christ has no body on earth but yours, no hands but yours, no feet but yours. Yours are the eyes through which Christ's compassion for the world is to look out; yours are the feet with which He is to go about doing good; and yours are the hands with which He is to bless us now." Single parents could certainly use extra hands and feet that are attached to loving hearts. Every time you relieve a single parent's physical weariness, you relieve a little of their mental and emotional weariness too.

Offer specific help. Telling the single parent, "Just let me know what you need," puts one more burden on an already overwhelmed person. Instead, ask what that parent's biggest challenges are, listen for the practical support they need, and then (prayerfully) offer specific help. Here are a few examples:

Saturday night we've got a sitter! We would love for you to come hang out with us. Drop your daughter at our house and let's get Mexican food. If it's okay with you, she can spend the night and we'll bring her to church with us Sunday.

Your toilet keeps backing up? My husband is great with plumbing. He can come by after dinner tonight and take a look at it if you want him to.

You can't make Tuesday morning small groups because you always drive your boys to school on Tuesdays? There's a Thursday evening group. Would that be an option?

You mentioned that money is tight. Is there something you need this week? I'd love to pay for groceries/basketball shoes/ the babysitter.

Be gentle with their pride (accepting help can be hard!), and don't make a big deal about any of it. If the single parent says no, fine. Offer again soon. More than anything, you are just trying to establish yourself as someone who wants to help when there's a need. If you are humble and low-key about it, the offer itself will be a gift. Confess and repent of any glory-seeking before you even open your mouth. You will humiliate them if you treat them as a service project, and God won't be impressed either.

Think creatively. Keep both parent and child in mind as you pray and ask God to show you where you might help. Whatever you do for the child helps the parent, and vice versa. What days of the year might be challenging? Some older teenage friends from church took my boys out for flag football and burgers on Christmas Eve so I could prepare the final surprises in peace (one of them even came back late at night and helped me build a drum set). What milestones are hard? Teaching kids to drive is both terrifying and a strain on the relationship. If God gave you nerves of steel, take a fledgling driver out for lessons and spare parent and child one more thing to fight about. (Be sure to show the child how to check tire pressure and change a flat while you're at it.) Offer to help shop for back-to-school clothes, remember the tough anniversaries, and show up for graduation.

If you are married with children, notice the times when you and your spouse have to divide and conquer. Those are the times when a single parent might be glad to accept an offer of help.

If you know the family well enough, your offers will be timely and meaningful.

Befriend a child. A friend from church asked what he might do for my seventeen-year-old son the summer before his senior year. After thinking it over, I came back with two situations I had been stressed about. I asked our friend to lead my son through the process of finding a summer job and to be a sounding board as he figured out what he wanted to do after graduation. This friend faithfully did both, hiring my son to work construction for the summer (hard labor and great experience) and then taking him out to lunch monthly. I certainly could have done both of those things, but my son gained a friend and heard wise counsel from someone other than me. Having another adult in the mix kept possible tension at a minimum for my son and me, allowing both of us breathing room to enjoy his senior year.

Celebrate special days. Children love to be able to celebrate their parents. Have your single friend's children over to make valentines. Take a child Christmas or birthday shopping for their mom or dad. Invite them to think about what their dad likes: Music? Books? Cool T-shirts? You will subtly teach them to see their parents as people, not just as mom or dad. I love books, so our friends built a little lending library for our front yard and helped my boys paint and install it.

For several years a friend made a tradition of taking my youngest son to Macy's jewelry counter the night before my birthday. She taught him to notice that I like earrings (and bargains), so the next day he would proudly present me with a couple of little boxes she had gift-wrapped, announcing, "Macy's has great stuff on clearance, Mom!" These simple kindnesses delight parents and kids more than you can imagine.

Offer literal rest. Show the single parent that they can pass you the baton. Depending on the age of the child(ren), you can play with a toddler while the parent takes a nap. Give a good book to a parent who seldom gets to read, and provide time for them to enjoy it. Take their children to your house for an overnight and keep them long enough to let the parent sleep in. If you feel ambitious, keep the kids for the weekend and let the single parent go out of town. If the parent shares custody, don't assume they get the rest they need when the kids are in their other parent's home, and don't assume they won't want to see you when they do have the kids. Sometimes the simple act of inviting another family to eat with yours offers a single parent more rest than you realize. Single parents find a measure of rest when they aren't the only adult around.

Fun can be the best help of all. If the single parent doesn't have to plan or execute the fun but can just show up and join in, you've given their whole family a gift.

Bearing the Burden of Prayer

Tonja didn't know where to turn. Her child's father continued his erratic and unsafe behavior with their daughter, but custody arrangements demanded she spend time with her dad. Her lawyer warned that full custody would be impossible, so with every legal dead end, Tonja grew more distraught and exhausted.

She went to a woman from her church for prayer. This woman prayed fervently for her and her daughter, that the blood of Jesus would surround and protect their little family. She went on to pray that the little girl would never have to see her father again and that God would be with them. Tonja left the prayer time feeling like this woman did not understand the way divorce worked, but she prayed in agreement anyway.

One week later Tonja received notice that she had been granted full custody of her daughter, along with permission to change her daughter's last name to match her own.

Tonja is still a single mom, still working seven days a week to provide for her daughter. She still feels overwhelmed and burned out some days, but she has hope. God is good, and her church family will carry her burdens to Jesus with her. She does not have to do everything alone.

When you support single-parent families in the ways mentioned in this chapter, you are accomplishing so much holy work. You lift some of the burden off the single parent, helping a dad or mom remember that they are not alone. You establish a relationship with a child who is missing the security of growing up with two trustworthy, reliable adults who love them and each other unconditionally and in all circumstances. You demonstrate for that child what the love of God expressed through his church looks like, planting seeds of servant-love that will bear fruit in their lives and in the lives of hurting children for generations to come.

six

God's Presence in Our Loneliness

*A father to the fatherless, a defender of widows,
is God in his holy dwelling.
God sets the lonely in families. (Psalm 68:5–6)*

I'm sitting alone on the couch, waiting for a teenager to come home from a night out with friends. I've heard the stories. I know what the temptations are—I was a teenager myself! As the clock ticks past curfew fifteen minutes, thirty minutes, an hour, I check my phone, I pace the floor, I wait. Am I angry? Afraid? Will the police come to the door to tell me there's been an accident? When he saunters in over an hour late, how do I react? There's no one to talk to, no one to reassure me, no one to help me decide how to handle it. I am alone.

He's missed so many days of school this month that we have asked the doctor to certify his illness so he won't be held back. No fever, no vomiting, just an ongoing headache and stomachache bad enough to keep him horizontal on the couch for almost two weeks. Every scary test comes back clean. There's no apparent medical reason that my child can't eat and can't go to school (which he loves). Do I keep pressing for more tests? Which tests? Which specialists? Or is this anxiety? Depression? How do I help? I have lost the other person who loves my child as much as I do. I am alone.

We have one last lunch together before I leave my oldest child at college. We walk over to a diner near campus and sit at a table for two, my son's back to the glass door. I can see over his shoulder to the sidewalk outside, where my son's new friend is saying goodbye to his family. He hugs his sister and gives a laughing high-five half-hug to his little brother. Then he turns to his mother, who is smiling bravely. His father wraps long arms around his wife and son and holds them tight, tears streaming down his face. The boy finally breaks away and waves goodbye. His parents and siblings watch him go, the father holding his wife under one arm and pulling the brother and sister under the other arm. My son will not get a tearful hug from his father. When he hugs me goodbye and walks away, I will stand alone.

I mentioned in the previous chapter that the first thing single parents tended to share with me in our interviews was how tired they were. But when I asked them to tell me the hardest thing about being a single parent, all of them talked about loneliness.

Loneliness is the dark thread that runs through all our single-parent struggles. Busyness cuts us off from time with other adults. Vulnerability makes us wonder who we can trust. Fear thrives in the vacuum created by a missing spouse. Pride keeps us from reaching out to admit we are lonely. Loneliness feels weirdly shameful, as if there is something wrong with us or we are ungrateful for our families. We have children to love who love us back. We have friends and a church that God tells us is our family. What right do we have to say we are lonely?

But loneliness is not merely an absence of people, it's an absence of closeness and commitment. Loneliness is the sense that although there are people around, I long for companions who are attuned to me, for the one who is "my person" and I am his. I miss feeling understood, seen, and known by someone who is devoted to me and my children above anyone else. I miss having the one who likes me best, the person who has to talk to me at parties and sit with me at the school play. I miss having a sounding board, someone to voice my thoughts and fears to, who will reassure me and disagree with me and help me refine what I think and why I think it. I miss having someone else to run the errand when I'm tired and someone who knows how I like my tea. I miss letting someone else worry about fixing the broken water heater or filing the taxes. I miss making the cookies he liked and buying his toothpaste.

Some, but not all, of this loneliness is the product of being unmarried. Depending on their circumstances, single parents often spend tons of time with their children, but there's not another adult around. Single parents who share custody have a kind of whiplash. When the kids are in their home, the single parent wants to focus on them, but that leaves no time for adult friends. When the kids go to their other home, the single parent misses them, worries about them, feels guilty for being relieved to have a break, and needs to connect with friends who may or may not be available to hang out when the single parent is finally free to do so. To complicate matters, children can be highly attuned to their single parent's moods and emotions, creating both an intense bond and a temptation to overshare. As single parents, we have to resist alleviating our loneliness by turning our children into the adult we miss having around.

Our married friends don't know what any of this feels like, which only makes us feel more alone.

All the Lonely People

The great irony here is that loneliness has reached epidemic proportions. For several years now, loneliness has been a hot topic of conversation, especially among public health officials who recognize that social isolation has serious physical and mental health consequences. Former Surgeon General Vivek Murthy wrote *Together: The Healing Power of Human Connection in a Sometimes Lonely World* to address the loneliness he saw affecting well-being across the United States. Britain established a new government post, the minister of loneliness, and gave the position a substantial budget to combat the isolation its citizens feel. Oddly enough, all of this comes at a time when we are more connected than ever by our smartphones, but somehow disembodied interactions don't provide the nurture our souls need. Loneliness garnered a lot of public attention even before the pandemic introduced the narrative that other people are bad for your health and that gathering with friends is at best foolish and at worst hostile and antisocial. COVID only added to our confusion about what it means to love your neighbor with embodied presence.

The cultural conversation around loneliness is in some respects an odd one, because we know the cure. Loving, intimate relationships, where people feel seen, known, and cared for, banish loneliness. But we seem to have forgotten how to have those relationships.

God Invites Intimacy; Sin Destroys It

For three years, Jesus lives in intimate fellowship with twelve disciples. With Jesus these men are free to be as open as they dare, asking their most sensitive questions and sharing their most personal fears and failings. Sure, there are squabbles and disagreements and a lot of jockeying for power, but with Jesus leading them, the intimacy and safety these men experience during their time together are transformative. Being fully known and fully loved prepares them to step into the leadership of the early Christian church, but first they fail the Lover of their souls, just as he knew they would.

All the disciples scatter when the Romans come to arrest Jesus, but the failures of Judas and Peter stand out. In betraying Jesus, Judas betrays all the people who love them both, but Judas's great loss is Jesus, who knows him best and loves him still. We cannot help but shudder at the eternal loneliness of a man who rejects not only the friendship of Jesus (as all sinners do, before God calls us to repentance) but also his saving grace. Peter betrays Jesus too, denying him three times, just as Jesus told him he would. Peter knows the loneliness of failure, of not living up to his own bold promises to stand by Jesus, of facing the weakness of his love for his Savior.

But no one has ever been lonelier than Jesus.

The Loneliness of Jesus on the Cross

Throughout the last week of Jesus's life, we see the chasm widen between him and his disciples, who repeatedly misunderstand when he tells them what will happen. Rather than grasp that he is marching toward his crucifixion, they think the moment of triumph is at hand, perhaps a coup d'état in the works. He enters Jerusalem surrounded by the praises of the people. He will leave it staggering under the weight of a wooden cross. During the last night of his life, the Lord of the universe tenderly washes his disciples' dirty feet (John 13:1–17), comforts them (14:1–4), and prays for their protection (17:11), all while knowing that every one of them will desert him when the Romans come for him. In the garden, he asks his closest friends, Peter, James, and John, to sit with him while he prays. "My soul is overwhelmed with sorrow to the point of death," he tells them. "Stay here and keep watch with me" (Matt. 26:38). Three times he discovers them asleep instead.

As painful as their failures must have been to Jesus, who has the tenderest heart there has ever been, nothing compares to the loneliness he will feel when his Father turns his face away. More than the rejection of his friends, more than the excruciating suffering of crucifixion, more than the weight of the sins of the world, this separation is what Jesus wants to avoid when he prays in the garden, "My Father, if it is possible, may this cup be taken from me" (Matt. 26:39). Jesus has spent eternity in perfect loving communion with his heavenly Father, never knowing a moment's distance in their mutual uninterrupted love and delight. We who love so imperfectly cannot imagine the loneliness Jesus willingly stepped into when he refused to avoid the cross, but we can hear the anguish in some of his last words: "My God, my God, why have you forsaken me?" (Matt. 27:46).

Psalm 22, which Jesus is quoting here, gives us insight into what this loneliness feels like for Jesus. He is bearing the guilt of the world on the cross, and yet his loneliness is so great it obscures everything but his desperation for the Father to come close again: "Why are you so far from saving me, so far from my cries of anguish?" (v. 1). His cries have no end because he has lost the rest he once enjoyed in God's loving presence (v. 2). God has faithfully answered Israel's cries for deliverance; Israel has not been put to shame, but Jesus has (vv. 4–5). Being scorned, despised, mocked, insulted—Jesus has suffered all of these, but it is the silence of God that he cannot bear. He has lost his Father's delight (v. 8). "There is no one to help" (v. 11).

Lonely single parent, Jesus knows how you feel. He lost the one who was dearest to him. He who once lived in the eternal sunshine of the Father's affection was banished from the Father's presence. His cries went unanswered. Like those of us whose most intimate relationship is now firmly in the past, he had nothing but the memory of "This is my beloved Son"; he would not hear those words on the cross. No one would come to help.

Jesus willingly stepped into that loneliness *for you*. He loves you so much that he chose to endure a far greater desertion so that you would never have to be forsaken by the Father as he was. His sacrifice does not take away the pain of your loneliness but can reassure you of how loved you are even in it. God will never turn his face from you, because he turned away from Jesus instead.

The separation Jesus endured created our present reality: he is always with us.

The Promise of His Presence

The NIV translation of Hebrews 13:5 reads, "Never will I leave you; never will I forsake you." As comforting as those words are, that translation does not capture the intensity of the original Greek, which offers *five* negatives regarding abandonment. The Amplified Bible helps us gain a fuller understanding of what Jesus is saying here.[1] "He has said, 'I will never [under any circumstances] desert you [nor give you up nor leave you without support, nor will I in any degree leave you helpless], nor will I forsake or let you down or relax My hold on you [assuredly not]!'" (Heb. 13:5 AMP).

Preacher Charles Spurgeon wrote about this verse:

It would hardly be possible in English to give the full weight of the Greek. We might render it, "He himself has said, I will never, never desert you, and I will never, never, never abandon you." . . . Two negatives nullify each other in our language. In the Greek, they intensify the meaning following one after another. . . . It means that in no one single instance will the Lord leave you, nor in any one particular will He leave you, nor for any reason will He leave you. If you have cast yourself upon His infinite power and grace, He will carry you to the end. Not only will He not desert you altogether, but He will not leave you even for a little while. He may seem for a small moment to hide His face from you, but He will still love you and still supply your needs.[2]

God couldn't be more emphatic: he is not going to leave you, ever, for any reason. He will not fall in love with someone else, grow tired of you, go to jail, disappear, succumb to addiction, or die. He has already died, for your sake, and he rose again so that by his Spirit he would never have to be apart from you. His commitment to you is nearly incomprehensible in its permanence and totality. The extent to which you can grasp this will determine how secure you feel in the love of God (Eph. 3:14–19).

To be forsaken is to be abandoned, left behind, or deserted. Our faithful heavenly Father knows we fear abandonment, rejection, and death because these can happen or have happened to us. Hear his compassion for us, and be "convinced that neither death nor life, neither angels nor demons, neither the present nor the future, nor any powers, neither height nor depth, nor anything else in all creation, will be able to separate us from the love of God that is in Christ Jesus our Lord" (Rom. 8:38–39).

As glorious and true as these verses are, the permanent presence of the Holy Spirit is very different from the imperfect (but warm and tangible) presence of a wife or a husband. With all due respect, the Holy Spirit does not drive carpool after band practice or reconcile the bank statement. Adam's loneliness in the garden is "not good" (Gen. 2:18), and he doesn't even have kids yet. When God commands the first couple to be fruitful and multiply, he places childbearing, and by implication childrearing, squarely in the context of marriage, the covenant God created to alleviate loneliness, nurture children, and typify Christ's union with his church. We who aren't married can learn to experience his presence as our spouse and co-parent through the ministry of the Holy Spirit.

Union with Christ: What God's Presence Means for Single Parents (and for All of Us)

God's promised presence means we are never alone. Regardless of what we feel, or how things appear, in Christ we truly will never be alone again. With the presence of the Holy Spirit, we enjoy the intimacy and commitment that we long for in a spouse. God stays near, not because he has to but because he wants to. It's his nature to love you. He is your Father, and in Christ you are his beloved child.

Again, it's sometimes hard to know how to experience his presence. Humans travel through this life in a body, and we experience the world in large part through our five senses. We encounter God's glory in creation—through music in worship, through the scent of gardenias on the breeze or the taste of buttery garlic bread, through the tiny, sweaty, trusting hand of a little child—but we can't see him with our eyes or hear his audible voice or reach out and touch him. He knows we have to learn to see him through the eyes of faith and hear his voice in the pages of our Bibles rather than experience him in the same way we experience other people. He has compassion for our weakness.

Though painful in some ways, being present with God in church community ministers to our yearning for him. Because we need tangible expressions of spiritual realities, Jesus gave us the sacrament of communion. Believers taste, smell, and receive the bread and wine, which we take into our bodies as a representation of our union with Christ. Music plays a key role too. Turning back to Psalm 22, we read in verse 3 that God *inhabits* the praises of his people (KJV). Other translations describe God as *enthroned* on the praises of believers (NIV, ESV). In either case, God is present in our united voices when we offer him our worship. The experience of singing together is both sensory—we see, hear, and feel God's body around us—and spiritual because music allows us to express and experience a reality beyond the power of words. Embodied worship ushers us into a limited (this side of heaven) but real unity with the Father and each other.

God's presence fills our ordinary days too. Centuries ago, a monk named Brother Lawrence came to believe that the key to contentment is found in what he called "practicing the presence of God," by which he meant that we can tune our souls to perceive God in the ways he can be seen and felt. Brother Lawrence believed the key was continual prayer: "Rejoice always, pray continually, give thanks in all circumstances; for this is God's will for you in Christ Jesus" (1 Thess. 5:16–18). He famously was assigned kitchen duty (which he hated) in the monastery where he lived, and he found great joy "practicing the presence" as he washed dishes. Switching to shoe repair later in life, Brother Lawrence continued his practice uninterrupted, and his fellowship with God grew deeper. His words in a letter to a friend might well be his advice to a single parent:

> I sympathize with your difficult situation. . . . But remembering God, praising Him, asking for His grace, offering Him your troubles, or thanking Him for what He has given you will console you all the time. During your meals or during any daily duty, lift up your heart to Him, because even the least little remembrance will please Him. You don't have to pray out loud; He's nearer than you imagine.[3]

Practice meditating on God's nearness often. Jesus gave his life so that we could be united to him: "I am in my Father, and you are in me, and I am in you" (John 14:20). That union is organic; we are as inseparable from and dependent on Christ as branches on a vine. The Holy Spirit lives in us. When we practice God's presence, we remain in him, and he remains in us (John 15:4). Though nothing will ever separate us from his love for us in Jesus (Rom. 8:38–39), we do make the choice to remain in his love when we stay attuned to and mindful of Jesus's love for us and our imperfect but growing love for him (John 15:9). This love bends our hearts toward obedience, and that obedience completes our joy (15:10–11).

While it is true that God's presence is not the same as a person's physical presence, God's presence satisfies like no one else's. Jerry Maguire would have us believe that another person can "complete" us, but God *actually does complete us*. He's the only one who can. Practicing his presence, you will enjoy—and that's the right word, *enjoy*—a far more personal, loving, committed intimacy with God than you ever could with another human being. No person can ever be as close to you as God is. No one will ever sacrifice more to be with you. No one will delight in you more than Father God does, and no one will delight you more. His love is better than life (Ps. 63:3). He makes his home in our hearts (Eph. 3:17). He is here to stay.

What This Means for the Church

"God sets the lonely in families" (Ps. 68:6) by adopting the lonely into his family.

The incomparable closeness we enjoy with God does not mean we can thrive without people. That's not gonna happen. God built us for fellowship with other people, as well as with himself

(Gen. 2:18). In community with other believers, we are "filled to the measure of all the fullness of God" (Eph. 3:19). If we want to grasp the width and length and height and depth of God's love, banishing our empty longings forever, we must do it together.

But as our loneliness epidemic makes clear, we've somehow lost sight of how to cultivate the kinds of relationships that take us to Jesus and nurture our souls. There's no better place than the church to relearn how to love each other well, because when church functions as God intended, it makes brothers and sisters of people who have no connection but Christ. He turns strangers into family.

This need applies to all of us—married people and singles need the church to be family too. Apart from Christ, human beings don't know how to sustain intimacy. Even the happiest married folk and the most contented singles know loneliness; sin has rendered this form of suffering universal. Feeling alienated, isolated, misunderstood, or rejected can happen to anyone. One day we will experience perfect fellowship, but in the meantime, we can learn and practice with those in our local church what it's like to live in right relationship. To the extent that we invest our attention and affection in Christ-centered community, we whet our appetites for heaven.

Hospitality

The easiest way to alleviate the loneliness of single-parent families is to hang out with them. Get to know both parents and children. Have meaningful conversations, and share something of yourself when you do. Spend time together. Develop give-and-take friendships so everyone benefits. It's truly that simple.

In one interview I had, a single-father pastor commented that one of the great challenges for churches is what he called the "the unexamined cultural shape of American Christianity." Hyperfocused on our individuality, we regard our Christian homes as sanctuaries for the nuclear family at the expense of biblical values like hospitality, close relationships, and community.

Dining at the home of a prominent Pharisee, Jesus redefined hospitality for all the guests to hear:

> Jesus said to his host, "When you give a luncheon or dinner, do not invite your friends, your brothers or sisters, your relatives, or your rich neighbors; if you do, they may invite you back and so you will be repaid. But when you give a banquet, invite the poor, the crippled, the lame, the blind, and you will be blessed. Although they cannot repay you, you will be repaid at the resurrection of the righteous." (Luke 14:12–14)

Inviting guests into your home has little to do with personal preferences. True hospitality extends belonging and provision to people who need it, not only people you already like. There is nothing transactional about hospitality; apparently, we are to go out of our way to find people who cannot repay the kindness.

Jesus isn't talking about entertaining; he is talking about genuine welcome that meets mutual needs. Don't fall prey to the Pinterest hype that sells hospitality as something lavish or expensive. When we moved to Colorado and knew no one, a family we met at a Bible study invited my kids and me to eat lunch with them every Wednesday. They did not have much extra, yet they shared everything they had. Most of their groceries came from a food pantry for low-income families. Making lunch, we would cut mold off bread and cheese and trim brown spots off fruit and veggies, and I usually brought something from my house too. Julie showed me what Christian mom-love looks like while we made crafts, played board games, and built snowmen. I can't imagine what our family would have lost if she had not welcomed us in, brown spots and all.

It's easy to find reasons not to invite friends to your home.

If your compulsion to have everything spotless before anyone darkens your door keeps you from having folks over, take that to God and ask him to show you why. My personal favorite excuse is that I am not a very good cook (I'm not), but that's no reason not to order a pizza or to serve mac and cheese and salad from a bag. Hospitality is about making people feel welcome, but that doesn't mean you have to offer a lavish spread or wait on folks hand and foot. If you know a single mom who loves to cook, you might buy the groceries, invite her over, and play with her kids so she can cook in peace. If you have a big backyard, invite a family over to play freeze tag and eat popsicles. You don't have to plan an event. Simply invite other people into what your family is doing and make them feel welcome by relaxing when they're over.

In her book *The Gospel Comes with a House Key*, Rosaria Butterfield writes, "Radically ordinary hospitality is this: using your Christian home in a daily way that seems to make strangers neighbors, and neighbors the family of God."[4] You aren't so much serving others as you are receiving friends into your regular day, because that's what people who are comfortable with each other do.

As you get to know them, demonstrate the familiarity that comes with a lot of time together. Learn any cultural differences and take those into account. Remember food allergies and plan around bedtimes. If you give your kids some small chores, give the visiting kids some chores too. Any of them can take out the trash or help dry the dishes. Paradoxically, people feel at home when they are treated more like family than guests.

Hospitality doesn't always have to be at a house either. If you can't invite folks over, you can meet for coffee or go for a walk. Hospitality has more to do with welcome than anything else. How can you make another person feel known, enjoyed, and delighted in? A mason jar full of flowers from your yard can be a treat for the single mom who doesn't get flowers. If you make a loaf of bread, make two and share one. If a parent or their child feels like you know and like them, you're on your way to genuine friendship.

The Lonely Times

Here's a by no means exhaustive list of times when single parents can be more vulnerable to loneliness.

Evenings feel long without an extra set of hands or a listening ear. Everyone is tired and tempers wear thin, even in two-parent households. There may not be much you can do to alleviate loneliness for single parents here, other than being aware that they might be feeling this way. Most of the time, they need face-to-face, unhurried companionship, but in the evenings, texting is a great way to care for people. Single parents often don't have someone to ask how their day was, or how the evening routines went, or what they'd like prayer for, so you can be that person who checks in. There won't be a head on the pillow next to theirs, but you can send them off to bed knowing that someone loves them and is thinking of them and their child.

Weekends are lonely times for single parents and their kids. Married friends disappear on the weekends, and single friends enjoy a flexibility that single parents don't have. When I asked a single dad what he would say to someone who wants to care for him and his family, he didn't have to think about his answer: "Invite us in. Open the door. Welcome us into your family. It's not hard."

Invite them into your weekend. Ask single parents over. Ask them what they want or need. Parents may feel torn, wanting time to focus on their children even as they dread the isolation of no adult interaction, so invite the whole family over. For children who divide their time between two households, offer a chance for them to get to know you and your family better. If the kids are with their other parent, include the single parent in your gatherings anyway. They can always say no. Never assume that a single adult (whether they have kids or not) would feel uncomfortable going out with couples. Excluding friends who are no longer or have never been married only intensifies their loneliness. The newly single parent feels like their own life doesn't fit anymore, so take every chance you can to reassure them they have not lost you too. And the longtime single parent needs to know you understand that their loneliness may ebb and flow.

Summer feels like a never-ending weekend. The support that parents get from the routines of school and church virtually disappears, and married-parent families retreat into their own little worlds. Invitations for fun and fellowship evaporate such that the single parent and their child endure more extended isolation than at any other time of year. The financial strain of summer childcare, the tension that comes with unrelieved togetherness, or the long stretches of separation mandated by custody arrangements can add up to increased stress, weariness, loneliness, and need.

Sundays can be tough. Sitting among the congregation, surrounded by families that look like what you wish your family looked like, is hard on both the parent and the child. The inward battle with envy and comparison is no fun, especially when you know you're supposed to be worshiping God with gratitude and rejoicing. The children do have the comfort of going to Sunday school with other kids, though the stories they hear about other families there can make them feel insecure about their own. In most churches, single parents have no place to go. Sunday school classes fill up with married couples and that feels weird for us, and we don't belong in the singles class. In my interviews I learned that single parents often hide out in the church library or an empty classroom during the Sunday school or small group hour. And more than one admitted to dropping their kids off and making a coffee run while they waited for the service to begin, just so they wouldn't have to figure out where to go.

After church can be particularly lonely for single-parent families. Butterfield writes that she and her husband

> remember what it was like . . . to have no place to go after worship, the odd tearing apart of the body of Christ as each retreats to his own corner or clique while the benediction still rings in the air. It is an act of violence and cruelty to the people in your church who routinely have no place to belong, no place to need and be needed, after worship. Worship leaves us full and raw, and we need one another.[5]

This makes Sundays after church ideal for invitations, either to your house or out to eat. It hurts to get in your car and head back into isolation after sharing in the worship of God. (This goes double for the parent who is in a challenging stretch with their kids, as with high-energy toddlers or crabby teenagers.) Almost no time of the week is more painful to be left out of a gathering, or to long for company, than Sunday lunch. The single parent may go years without much physical rest on the Sabbath, but you can offer them rest in being known and loved.

Special occasions and holidays can hurt too. Single parents often endure significant heartache when they are alone at graduation, a birthday, or the Fourth of July, not to mention Thanksgiving, Easter, and Christmas. The loneliness they feel on evenings and weekends intensifies over holiday weekends, which typically last longer and carry higher expectations and more emotional weight. Be aware of custody arrangements so you know when your single-parent friend will be missing their children. Busyness, money, strained family relations, travel—these things that stress you will be even more stressful for the single parent juggling everything solo, but nothing hurts like feeling isolated, invisible, and alone.

Things change over the years. Kids grow up. A mom who was never free to watch college football when her kids were little might find herself free every fall Saturday once her children start driving. A dad who rarely had his kids around when they were little may have more time with them when they are older. Just like anyone, single parents have seasons of greater and lesser loneliness. Tell them the things that make you feel lonely—caring for aging parents, a rebellious teenager, a tough work situation—and help them see that you need their friendship as much as they need yours.

Finally, remember that single parents will need some *solitude*. Solitude recharges; loneliness depletes. Solitude gives room to breathe; loneliness craves connection. Knowing whether your single-parent friend is an introvert or an extrovert will help, but even the most extroverted parent appreciates time alone with their thoughts, or at least a little space from the incessant chatter of a curious four-year-old. The introverted single parent longs for quiet and may feel guilty for it. If you don't know whether your single-parent friend needs connection or solitude, just ask. Maybe she likes to garden or he likes to golf. Maybe he or she wants to grocery shop alone for once. How can you help them find time for solitude? In any case, don't be offended if they don't want to hang out sometimes (remember: they are exhausted); keep the invitations coming.

Keep an Eye on the Kids

The loneliness of kids in single-parent families is well documented. Though they may not want to acknowledge it or talk about it, these kids often feel different from other kids, especially in settings where both parents are expected to be present: church, recitals, performances, ball games, awards ceremonies, and such. They often miss the absent parent, whether or not the relationship is or was a warm one. In other cases, they dread knowing that both parents will be there. Whether the parents are cordial or hostile to each other, children feel caught between loyalties. Having other adults around can be a helpful buffer. Save a seat for the parent who is going to attend parents' night at the school alone. By all means, if you know a solo parent cannot make an important event, attend for the child's sake. Being there after the performance with a small grocery-store bouquet or giving a ride home after a tough loss helps the child feel less lonely.

Often children will have trouble naming their emptiness as loneliness. For the child who only ever lived in a home with one parent, they may wonder how they can be lonely for a parent they never really had. For others, the disruption that follows a divorce or a death can leave a child terribly lonesome. They may not have much time with a noncustodial parent; they may feel betrayed or confused by the change in their parents' relationship; their mom or dad may have to work longer hours than before. They may feel weird around the sibling who suddenly starts acting out or the sibling who seems unaffected by the changes. Lonely kids may feel they don't have anyone to talk to. It's possible to devote a lot of time and attention to a hurting child without ever creating the closeness that will help them feel seen and known. One man I interviewed felt loved by his youth pastor's presence after his parents divorced, but no one ever asked him to talk about what had happened to their marriage or how he felt about it.

Certainly you'll mediate your relationship with a child through their parent, but kids need what adults need: true connection and friendship.

Just Be a Friend

When my husband died, one of his best friends began taking my youngest son out to breakfast every Friday morning before school. At the time, my son was in third grade, and they continued their breakfasts until my son was in tenth grade, when they switched to weekly suppers. Once a week my son got a greasy breakfast feast to delight the heart of any growing boy, plus a large Dr Pepper that I would never have given him.

But more than that, my son had the steady presence of a man who enjoyed him, prayed with him, asked good questions, listened to his answers, and told him he loved him through both word and action. To this day that friend would insist he gets more out of their hangouts than my son does. They're still great friends. Nothing fancy, just commitment, time, and a lot of bacon.

Doesn't that sound like fun?

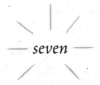

God's Protection in Our Vulnerability

I love you, Lord, my strength.

The Lord is my rock, my fortress and my deliverer;
my God is my rock, in whom I take refuge,
my shield and the horn of my salvation, my stronghold.

I called to the Lord, who is worthy of praise,
and I have been saved from my enemies. (Psalm 18:1–3)

A bruised reed he will not break,
and a smoldering wick he will not snuff out. (Isaiah 42:3)

After her daddy left, her grandparents brought her to church every Sunday because her mom didn't care to see people whispering about their family. Still, she loved getting dressed up and singing songs and hearing about Jesus from the pastor her grandparents admired so much.

Which is why she trusted the pastor when he invited her into his office and shut the door behind her. At age thirteen, she was smart enough to know there was no reason for him to slide the lock into place when she stepped in after him, so she was bewildered until she heard pounding on the office door. An elder had spotted the whole thing and immediately made a scene in the hall until the pastor opened the door and let her out. She was physically unharmed but did not know what to make of a man who preached Jesus's love the same morning he preyed on a young girl.

This girl's nightmare could happen to any child. Her near miss with a sexual predator did not happen as a direct result of her father leaving the family, but her distance from her father (and, on Sunday mornings, her mother) did leave her more exposed to the possibility.

The Vulnerability of the Single-Parent Family

It's fair to say that single mothers experience vulnerability more than single fathers, and many are susceptible to financial trouble. Coupled with the fact that we earn less, women are more likely to be taken advantage of than men when it comes to making major purchases or home repairs. Not long ago I needed a new roof, and every company that gave me an estimate wanted to know what my husband thought of their price. I did not tell them I don't have a husband. Perhaps none of them would have tried to overcharge me, but I didn't plan to give them an opportunity.

Single mothers have to learn to think defensively. One single mother I know has made a career of empowering other single mothers to develop and manage financial plans for their families. It's one more fight for the already exhausted single mom who has to wonder whom she can trust to give her a fair price, do good work, and tell her the truth. No one wants to be paranoid, but we cannot afford to abandon caution. Tasks that single fathers are more likely to struggle with—juggling work, cooking, cleaning, playdates, doctor's appointments, and carpooling—are vital to their kids' thriving, but these issues don't represent danger to financial stability.

This feeling of vulnerability is something single parents have a hard time explaining to people who aren't raising children alone. It's not as if the now-absent spouse sat by the door all night with a shotgun to protect the home from intruders. But as every Christian knows, we live in a spiritual war zone. Protecting our kids from sin within and evil without feels doubly hard for the solo mom or dad.

The Bible is full of verses about God being our refuge, our stronghold, and our fortress. The word translated "refuge" in the NIV is used over forty times in the psalms alone. The metaphor of refuge acknowledges that the threats against our families are real and potent. We long to know that our children's physical bodies, emotional well-being, mental health, and above all their eternal destinies are secure. Prosperity preachers would like us to believe God dissolves every threat and pours out material blessing on every believer, but Scripture tells us otherwise. Jesus doesn't sugarcoat anything: "In this world you will have trouble" (John 16:33). He is speaking to the disciples, so we know he does not magically erase danger from the Christian life. We need look no further than Jesus's crucifixion to see that evil goes on offense against believers, and sometimes it appears as if evil has won.

Having kids makes us feel that much more vulnerable. Most parents would do *anything* to keep their child safe. As a married mother, I certainly prayed for my children's salvation and safety and health because, intellectually at least, I knew those things came from God. Becoming a single mom lent a new desperation to my protective instincts. I had relied on the partnership between my husband and me, standing shoulder to shoulder, to recognize danger and shield our children from it. When he was alive, we didn't feel so exposed. I didn't know how dependent I was on our team of two until it was only me to stand between my children and the big, bad threatening world.

And when it was just me, the world felt way bigger and badder. I imagined myself as Elastigirl—a.k.a. Mrs. Incredible—who could cover her children with her body like a bubble (or transform herself into a boat or a parachute or a shield) and rescue them from danger, but I felt far from being a superhero. But having God as our refuge is like this. He gives us exactly what we would have asked for if we knew everything he knows.

Experiencing God as our refuge transforms the single parent's mama- or papa-bear desperation into tentative trust and, eventually, deeper rest.

God Protects the Vulnerable

Psalm 91 describes God's protection, and Psalm 18 shows how fiercely he comes to our rescue.

> Whoever dwells in the shelter of the Most High
>   will rest in the shadow of the Almighty.
> I will say of the LORD, "He is my refuge and my fortress,
>   my God, in whom I trust." (Ps. 91:1–2)

Take a look at the verbs in verse 1, *dwell* and *rest*. We live in the shelter and the shadow of God. We set up camp there and are wise not to move from it. We have to be pretty close to something to be in its shadow, so to dwell in the shelter God offers us, we need to draw close to him in every way we know how. If you become anxious or fearful, it's a clue that you have wandered away from God's shadow. God's presence covers your time in prayer and in his Word, but it also shades his church and his people in it.

In verse 2, the psalmist coaches himself on how to pray. We train our mouths to say and our thoughts to affirm, *I trust God. He is my refuge.* No person, no job, no bank account can be a refuge for me and my kids. Only God can. It's personal: God is *my* God, *my* refuge, *my* fortress. And because he is for me, he is for my kids too.

> Surely he will save you
>> from the fowler's snare
>> and from the deadly pestilence.
> He will cover you with his feathers,
>> and under his wings you will find refuge;
>> his faithfulness will be your shield and rampart.
> (vv. 3–4)

A fowler lures birds with carefully chosen bait to capture them (v. 3). This is how evil works; our temptations are personalized so that the Enemy can hold us captive. When we feel vulnerable, we are liable to seek shelter in a false refuge like a new spouse or a higher-paying job (which are potentially good things, just not saviors). When we put our trust in these things rather than in God, we find ourselves trapped.

The depiction of God as a bird (v. 4) is an image Jesus later echoes when describing the way he wants to shield the city of Jerusalem: "Jerusalem, Jerusalem, you who kill the prophets and stone those sent to you, how often I have longed to gather your children together, as a hen gathers her chicks under her wings, and you were not willing" (Matt. 23:37). The image of Jesus as a mother bird longing to draw her chicks close shows us Jesus's tenderness toward the defenseless. The bird draws her babies close out of love and for protection. Under her wings she shelters her defenseless chicks from a storm, or from the hot sun, or from an enemy swooping in to eat them. The mother does by instinct what Jesus was about to do when he uttered those words over Jerusalem: he put himself between us and danger. He made himself vulnerable in order to protect us.

At the cross, the chief priests call out to Jesus to save himself. But if he had called legions of angels to his defense, you and I would have been lost. Jesus stayed and took the wrath of God so that we wouldn't have to. The protection that God offers in this psalm is not only protection from the dangers of this world. He does protect us from illness and car accidents and financial disaster and relationship ruin, probably far more often than we know. But he is far more interested in protecting us from the enemy of our souls.

Psalm 91 goes on to describe the battlefield we live in. It is terrifying, dark, and riddled with thousands of flying arrows, the air thick with stalking disease (vv. 5–7). And yet, in Jesus, we don't need to be afraid. Colossians tells us why: "You have been raised with Christ. . . . For you died, and your life is now hidden with Christ in God" (3:1, 3). Because we are hidden in Christ, we have already died to sin and have been raised with Christ. We will still suffer and die (unless Jesus returns first), but we have nothing to fear because we are hidden in Christ (Col. 3:3).

> For he will command his angels concerning you
> to guard you in all your ways;
> they will lift you up in their hands,
> so that you will not strike your foot against a stone.
> (Ps. 91:11–12)

Is God really promising that we will not stub our toes?

Satan tries to twist this verse to make it say so. In Matthew 4, quoting this exact verse, Satan tempts Jesus to throw himself off the high temple wall and to use God's promise of protection like a magic trick. Jesus does not take that bait because he knows better than to test God. Similarly, we can be tempted to use God's promise here to mean he will never let harm befall us or our children, and that simply does not line up with God's Word. Part of our call as believers is to know God's Word well and to listen for the Spirit so we can discern what Scripture means and does not mean. God does not promise that we will not suffer. He does promise that he will be with us in our pain and use it for our good (Rom. 8:28).

In Psalm 18 David describes God's response when one of his children cries for help. Running from Saul, so close to death he can virtually feel himself tangled in its cords (v. 4), David calls to God for help, and God responds immediately. What thrills David (and any believer) is God's wrath on behalf of his endangered child. As God moves toward rescue, the earth trembles and quakes (v. 7). Smoke and fire, thunder and lightning, hail and darkness accompany our angry heavenly Father as he makes war on his child's enemy (vv. 8, 11–14). The rescue itself is a picture of tenderness:

> He reached down from on high and took hold of me;
> he drew me out of deep waters.
> He rescued me from my powerful enemy,
> from my foes, who were too strong for me.
> They confronted me in the day of my disaster,
> but the LORD was my support.
> He brought me out into a spacious place;
> he rescued me because he delighted in me. (vv. 16–19)

Hear the confidence in David's voice. God's delight is not reserved only for David. God delights in you, too, and in your child. Whatever threatens your family angers him, and you can be sure that he will move heaven and earth to be your strength, your rock, your fortress, and your deliverer (vv. 1–2). In Christ, he already has.

What This Means for the Church

As we saw in the introduction, studies demonstrate that single-parent families are more vulnerable to a host of life-altering problems than two-parent families are. But statistics aren't destiny, especially where the Holy Spirit is involved. God covers vulnerable families with special protection, and he expects his church to do the same. He means business: "Do not take advantage of the widow or the fatherless. If you do and they cry out to me, I will certainly hear their cry. My anger will be aroused, and I will kill you with the sword; your wives will become widows and your children fatherless" (Ex. 22:22–24). Our God expects us to fight for justice for the most vulnerable. God help the Christian guilty of either exploitation or neglect.

No matter what the context looks like, anyone can offer presence and support. What matters most is giving oneself in genuine love and Christian character. If you have a certain skill, share your expertise. Be the person whom the single parent can trust to keep their children or help with closely guarded personal information. Be the person they can call in an emergency. You protect single parents and their children by being trustworthy.

Regarding financial vulnerability, if you work in finance, accounting, or banking, help parents who need it. Be the person who can interpret a tax bill or untangle complicated alimony issues and do it with discretion, tact, and kindness. If you have medical training, you can be a sounding board or an advocate for the parent navigating health issues alone. If at all possible, give your services for free, and thank God you have the knowledge to share.

Regarding money, which is never easy to talk about, do the single parents you know have enough money to pay their bills? Buy groceries? Can they afford to buy their kids the supplies they need for school? What about single parents you don't know (yet)? Can you connect families in your community with those who administer mercy funds at your church? With much prayer and the tact that comes from humility, how can you share what God has given you with families in financial need?

Home and car repairs and yard work are daunting for parents

who have not had to handle those before. Let's be honest—newly single moms usually have not been responsible to keep the cars tuned up. You can help. A church in Texas hosts a monthly car-tune-up day for single mothers. A member of the congregation owns a shop where single parents can come for maintenance and checkups at a fraction of the cost and know they aren't being taken for a (figurative) ride. I have relied on church friends for help with a broken air conditioner, multiple leaky showers, and a mold problem (among other things). I knew I could trust them. Similarly, some newly single parents have not been involved with cooking and cleaning. Maybe they need meal support or help with the chores. You can offer to teach the newly single parent to do household chores, you can share the meal you made for your own family, or you can do the work for them.

Another way you can protect vulnerable single parents and their children is in your conversations. Don't talk about them behind their backs. Sometimes prayer time can veer into gossip, where confidences are shared in the name of "let's pray." Allow the mom or dad to do the sharing if they choose; otherwise, keep your spoken prayers general: "We lift up the Harris family this week." You can pray about details silently, and if you don't know the details, God does.

Pastors, be aware that normal church practices can leave a parent or child feeling exposed. A ministry leader shared the story of a single mother who started visiting their church with her child. After several months, this mom wanted to join the church but confessed that she still felt an obstacle. New members typically joined by going forward at the end of the service, and this mother did not feel comfortable standing in front of the congregation with her child, without a husband. Another church protected a family by holding a private infant dedication while the baby's parents were enmeshed in a contentious divorce. They allowed the mother's family and the father's family to remain in separate rooms while still honoring each parent's equal commitment to the baby. We the church can work to observe these important milestones in a manner that is biblically faithful and sensitive to the needs of the family. Every church should be vigilant to protect every child from predators. Be thankful for the red tape of child protection policies, don't grumble about the training, and remember that man-made programs aren't foolproof. Be vigilant on behalf of every child, as the elder in our story was. If caring for children is your gift, by all means share that gift with single parents in every way you can, and make every effort to keep their children as safe as you would your own.

In every circumstance, protect the dignity of the single parent you are offering to help. It bears repeating: these families are not service projects, they are people. Avoid the language of "serving" altogether: you are simply loving your neighbor.

A Word for Church Leaders

For pastors and church leaders, connecting need with expertise is an ongoing challenge. Relationships—true, connected, spiritual friendship among brothers and sisters adopted by God's grace into his family—will always be more effective than programs. You are already working to foster connection between the people in your pews. They pass the peace during the service. They pray for one another. Remind them in your teaching that God has made them family, and show them what this means by creating community in small groups, sharing meals and celebrations, and serving the larger community alongside one another. The possibilities are as endless and varied as individual congregations. Pray and seek God's guidance. Keep issuing invitations and offering opportunities for loving, mutual relationships to thrive.

Sometimes these relationships grow as people connect in church ministries and programs. Logistics will vary from context to context. A very small congregation in rural Iowa probably will not have the personnel or finances (or need) to construct an entire program of support for single parents, but it might be able to keep a notebook in the church office where members can catalog the kinds of help they can offer. Or a well-organized lay leader can connect helpers with families, which also helps members grow in relationship and affection. Down the road, a megachurch in Chicago will certainly have resources and may even be able to hire a pastor tasked with connecting needs to support. The challenge for the larger congregation is developing true friendship between members so that help does not become more transactional than relational.

Service grows out of love more than the other way around, and to love people, we have to get to know them. Anytime a parent or child becomes a project rather than true family in Christ, we offer service that is less healing than it could be. Recall the single mother from the earlier chapter on single-parent families and the American church. She couldn't participate in women's ministry events because she couldn't afford a babysitter and was embarrassed to admit it. She didn't know the church had the money to help her; the church didn't know of her lack. It took a neighbor (who belonged to another church) to ask the right questions and connect this woman to her own congregation. Because he took the time to know her and build relationship, the neighbor became more trustworthy to this single mother than the people in her own church.

Churches and Families Are God's Provision for the Vulnerable

For a long time Reggie dodged the call he felt when he read James 1:27: "Religion that God our Father accepts as pure and faultless is this: to look after orphans and widows in their distress." To this day he jokes that it might have been easier to find a widow to take care of, but God led Reggie to adopt a teenage boy out of foster care. This son convinced Reggie that his deepest desire was to be a big brother, so Reggie adopted another son three years later . . . who also wanted to be a big brother. Ten years later, Reggie is a single dad to three young men who hear the gospel every day in their safe and loving home.

Each son came to him carrying the trauma of abuse and neglect, but Reggie keeps it simple, reading psalms together on the drive to school and praying together about whatever comes up during the day. He knows they need female discipleship, too, so he has been proactive about finding older women to disciple his sons so that each experiences the nurture of a godly woman. One of his sons has befriended a god-grandmother (as he calls her) named Miss Myra at church. She teaches Reggie's son to work in her garden and fix things around her house. After the hard work, they bake brownies together and dance around the kitchen table while they wait for the oven timer to ring. Miss Myra prays with the boy and answers his questions about Scripture, and the three of them eat fresh treats when Reggie comes to pick him up.

Before I became a single mom, verses about God as a rock and refuge and fortress seemed to apply to some distant biblical character who lived with the constant threat of war and disease and famine, or perhaps some embattled Christian in a society hostile to their beliefs. Becoming aware of my family's vulnerability deepened my appreciation for our protective heavenly Father. My boys and I have experienced his sheltering in community in ways that have strengthened our belonging.

eight

God's Wisdom in Our Uncertainty

The fear of the LORD is the beginning of wisdom. (Proverbs 9:10)

You must serve faithfully and wholeheartedly in the fear of the LORD. (2 Chronicles 19:9)

If any of you lacks wisdom, you should ask God, who gives generously to all without finding fault, and it will be given to you. (James 1:5)

My friend Paul knew that finding a new church for his family would not be easy, but he wasn't comfortable continuing at the church they attended before the divorce. After his wife left the marriage, he took his three kids to several churches, anticipating that, before long, Sunday mornings would deteriorate into yet another struggle. He needed wise counsel, and without a church home, he wasn't sure where to find it.

The hardest part, he said, was sitting in the car before the service. "You pull into the parking lot, and you're fighting the projected dialogue," the probing conversations he anticipated having with church members who wondered why he was walking in with his kids and without a wife. He would enter the sanctuary doors fighting vague dread and drive away afterward with a sigh of relief. Committed to finding a place for his family to worship, Paul was at a loss to know *how* to find a church that would care for all four of them in the wake of divorce. All the weight of his kids' spiritual discipleship landed squarely on his shoulders.

As I look back on discussions my husband and I had when we made decisions for our family, I wish I had now even half the confidence in my own opinion that I had when I was married. When I was married, I usually thought I knew what was best. But without Jeff here to hash things out or disagree with me, I question myself every day.

Having a partner as invested in your family's well-being as you are is a comfort that married parents don't know they have until they lose it. Even when my husband frustrated and annoyed me, I could trust his love for our kids. He was never careless or thoughtless when it came to our sons.

But while married parents can rely on each other's wisdom and make decisions together, this luxury can lead to prayerlessness. Without even realizing it, married parents can be lulled into a false sense of security by their joint wisdom and leave the Lord out of decisions altogether.

Single parents find seeking God's wisdom a necessity, a first step rather than a fallback, when they have to make decisions for their family.

God Guides Jehoshaphat

The Old Testament king Jehoshaphat models how believers can both ask for and receive wisdom from the Lord. Jehoshaphat is one of the godlier kings of Judah. While he wrestles with sin like anyone else, this king commits to seeking the Lord first as he rules over his people. Whether he's conducting the ordinary business of governing or facing threats to the nation's security, the fear of the Lord is consistently the beginning of Jehoshaphat's wisdom (Prov. 9:10). Instructing a cohort of newly installed judges, Jehoshaphat lays the foundation for their leadership: "You must serve faithfully and wholeheartedly in the fear of the LORD" (2 Chron. 19:9). Later, his mettle is tested when he receives news that a vast army is assembling against Judah. Rather than calling a council of generals and marshaling his considerable wealth to prepare for war, Jehoshaphat decides to inquire of the Lord, and he declares a national fast to prepare all the people to receive God's direction. His leadership unites the citizens of Judah: "The people of Judah came together to seek help from the LORD; indeed, they came from every town in Judah to seek him" (2 Chron. 20:4).

Standing before the assembled people, Jehoshaphat prays. He begins by declaring God's sovereign power and their nation's intimate history with God's goodness:

> LORD, the God of our ancestors, are you not the God who is in heaven? You rule over all the kingdoms of the nations. Power and might are in your hand, and no one can withstand you. Our God, did you not drive out the inhabitants of this land before your people Israel and give it forever to the descendants of Abraham your friend? (2 Chron. 20:6–7)

As he praises God, Jehoshaphat reminds the people that God's character encompasses both unlimited power and ongoing covenant relationship, established centuries before in his friendship with Abraham. God in heaven is the almighty source of all the strength in the universe (and strength is what Judah will need to fight this approaching army), and yet he deigned to befriend a mere man and bless his innumerable descendants (Gen. 22:18). Jehoshaphat's prayer marvels at God's majesty and God's humility all at once, orienting the hearts of the people to see God rightly, and to see themselves in relation to this incomparable, paradoxical, sovereign Lord. According to Tim Keller, the fear of the Lord does not mean we are afraid of him; rather, fearing God is "sustaining a joyful astonished awe and wonder before Him."[1] Jehoshaphat sustains that awe through prayer, praise, and acknowledgment of his dependence on God's understanding rather than his own. Fearing God opens Jehoshaphat to receive the wisdom God has for him as he makes decisions about how to care for his threatened people.

Fear of the Lord then makes it possible for Judah to accept and trust God's will, no matter what comes next:

> If calamity comes upon us, whether the sword of judgment, or plague or famine, we will stand in your presence before this temple that bears your Name and will cry out to you in our distress, and you will hear us and save us. (2 Chron. 20:9)

This is not an easy prayer. Jehoshaphat is not being glib here; he knows the threat his people are facing. His faith does not render him ignorant or unafraid. As parents praying for our children, we don't express this kind of trust lightly either. God may not lift a child's depression, even if we prayerfully choose to pursue counseling or medical treatment. We may lose the house, the car, or the job, even though we prayed and followed God's direction the best we knew how. Experience tells us the worst may happen anyway: The marriage fell apart. The husband found another woman. The wife died. The addict couldn't stay clean. Calamity can and does come, and sometimes there is the "sword of judgment" in it.

And yet God "will hear us and save us."

Jehoshaphat was confident in God's desire and power to save them, even if their worst nightmare came true. His words echo the declaration of Shadrach, Meshach, and Abednego, who refused to worship any idol or man even if God did not save them from the roaring furnace (Dan. 3:16–18). Likewise, even as many of the disciples fell away, Peter declined to leave Jesus's side, saying, "Lord, to whom shall we go? You have the words of eternal life" (John 6:68). This is audacious, counterintuitive, foolish-to-the-world trust. The idea that we cry out for help to the very one who appears to have let us down means we must somehow believe he is wiser and more loving than our limited perspective can comprehend.

What is most remarkable about these declarations of faith? These men made these claims *before* Jesus died on the cross. From our post-resurrection vantage point, we can look to the cross for irrefutable proof that God can redeem the most unjust, most hopeless, most tragically needless situations imaginable. We can trust him even when we have no idea how he will bring good from our tragedy (Rom. 8:28). Never in history was hope more irrevocably lost than when Jesus breathed his last and gave up his spirit, yet even at a time so dark that the sun refused to shine, God was working unspeakable glory for our good, for your good, and for the good of your child.

So while disaster may come, King Jehoshaphat knows how to respond: his people will cry out to God. God will hear, and God will save. Even if their worst comes to pass, God is their only rescuer and redeemer. This is the safety we have when we make decisions for our families. Even if he is trembling with fear as he speaks the words, this kind of trust is what enables Jehoshaphat to pray,

> For we have no power to face this vast army that is attacking us. *We do not know what to do, but our eyes are on you.* (2 Chron. 20:12, italics mine)

In that truth, all the men, women, and children of Judah stand before the Lord and wait expectantly for his response.

Reading through 2 Chronicles 20 for the whole story, note the recurrence of the word *stand*. Jehoshaphat *stands* before the assembly of the people at the temple, his feet resolutely planted in what he knows about God's character (v. 5). Taking a literal stand, he sets the example for his people—come what may, "we will *stand* in your presence before this temple that bears your Name" because no matter what happens, that is the safest, strongest place they can be (v. 9). After the prayer, the nation *stands* together, ready to wait and ready to move, depending on what God tells them (v. 13). And what does God tell them? Through his Spirit speaking through the prophet Jahaziel, he says, "The battle is not yours, but God's. . . . Take up your positions; *stand firm* and see the deliverance the LORD will give you. . . . Do not be afraid, do not be discouraged" (vv. 15, 17, italics mine). The people fall on their faces in thanksgiving, but then the worship leaders *stand* up and praise God "with a very loud voice" (v. 19). And on the morning of the battle that God is going to fight for them, Jehoshaphat *stands* once again before the people and encourages them to "have faith in the LORD your God" (v. 20).

Jehoshaphat shows his people, and us, how to wait expectantly for the wisdom we need from the Lord. Judah stands so firmly dependent on the Word of the Lord that they show up to battle against a mighty army with nary a weapon in hand, unless you count their voices lifted in song. With his "feet fitted with the readiness that comes from the gospel of peace" (Eph. 6:15), Jehoshaphat prepares to move when and if he is told to move, or to stand still if that be the wisdom he is given. Here is a king who does not know what to do to protect his people but who is humble enough to ask for wisdom in front of them and to stand in expectation of receiving it.

What This Means for the Single Parent

Moms and dads don't lead nations (praise God), but we do lead colicky babies, high-maintenance toddlers, and kids with special needs, health issues, and learning disabilities, not to mention rebellious teenagers. Daily, even hourly, we need wisdom for life-changing choices (Do I send my son to live with his father?) and seemingly inconsequential ones (Is it wrong to let my kids watch TV during dinner so I can have some peace?). Jehoshaphat's prayer can be ours: *We do not know what to do, but our eyes are on you.*

Like Jehoshaphat, we can pray this prayer in front of the people we lead—our kids. Knowing when and how to let kids see us lean on the Lord requires wisdom. Children in single-parent homes worry about the parent they rely on most: Will he be there when I need him? Will she know what to do? All three of my sons worried about what would happen to them if I died too. They already felt vulnerable, and I wanted to reassure them that our home was safe and stable. At the same time, I wanted to be honest with them that while I often lacked wisdom, I trusted that God would give it if I asked.

So while we shouldn't let our kids in on all our prayers and struggles, it's crucial to lead our children to find wisdom in fearing God, not in following us. We are to carefully discern the age- and personality-appropriate ways to pray as a family so that we allow our children to see us taking our deepest needs to the Lord without frightening them unnecessarily. Jehoshaphat boldly revealed his uncertainty in front of the nation, so the people certainly could have exploited his vulnerability for their own gain. The people of Judah already knew they were in danger, and our kids often know what threatens our families too (sometimes they see it more clearly than we do). Pretending otherwise borders on dishonesty.

If we want to disciple our children to love and trust Jesus, we need to let them join in some of our vulnerable prayers so they can see him answer us. Because Jehoshaphat shared his need and uncertainty, praying together with the nation, he also shared with them the praise, the victory, and the plunder when God delivered them from their enemy (2 Chron. 20:24–28). This story has become part of the shared history of all believers, a testimony we rely on even today as we read about it. As you pray with your children and they see God move, your stories will become part of your family's testimony to God's faithfulness.

What This Means for the Church and the Single Parent, Together

Notice that Jehoshaphat is not Judah's only leader. Rather than giving the words of wisdom directly to Jehoshaphat, "the Spirit of the LORD came on Jahaziel" and "he stood in the assembly" (2 Chron. 20:14; there's our word *stand* again). God speaks to the nation through Jahaziel, his words echoing God's words to Moses when Israel was trapped against the Red Sea with the Egyptian army bearing down on them. The point is not to tell the people that God will save them the same way he did before—that first time, he parted the sea to drown an army, and this time, he will ambush the enemy while his people praise—but rather to remind the assembled nation of God's consistent character. God saves his people because they cannot save themselves. Rather than insisting he be God's sole instrument, the king is humble enough to bow down and worship the Lord in gratitude while God uses another man to instruct Judah.

While God certainly responds to our private prayers for wisdom, he often leads his church to seek him together and receive wisdom together, by the Holy Spirit and through each other. Every word is addressed to Judah corporately. They fast together, assemble as one nation, and pray together. Jahaziel prophesies over Jehoshaphat and "all who live in Judah and Jerusalem" (2 Chron. 20:15) so that they receive instruction and encouragement as a group, which leads them to worship together and, finally, to go into battle together, armed with songs of praise.

What was true for them is still true for us. Regardless of marital status or whether they have kids, mature believers seek God together and receive his guidance together.

When combined, three proverbs show us what this looks like, practically speaking:

> Plans fail for lack of counsel,
> > but with many advisers they succeed. (Prov. 15:22)

> Listen to advice and accept discipline,
> > and at the end you will be counted among the wise.
> > (Prov. 19:20)

> As iron sharpens iron,
> > so one person sharpens another. (Prov. 27:17)

We start by being open and honest with each other about our struggles. "Many advisers" indicates asking for help, and not from only one wise person. We believers need not fear; our belonging and righteousness are secure in Christ, so it's okay to admit we don't know what to do. Other people cannot advise and support us if we don't tell them what our problems look like. If we don't, we are left to our own devices, which may be what got us in trouble in the first place. And we miss out on the comfort of sharing our struggles and maybe helping someone else with their own.

In his excellent little book *Just Do Something*, Kevin DeYoung writes,

> For most of our decisions we would do well to simply ask someone else, "What do you think?" We spend all this time asking God, "What's Your will?" when He's probably thinking, "Make

a friend, would you? Go talk to someone. There's a reason I've redeemed a lot of you—because you do fewer dumb things when you talk to each other. Get some advice. You just might hear My voice."[2]

Ask a couple of trusted friends for wisdom and prayer, and be discerning. Don't go to the people-pleasing pal who always tells you what you want to hear or to the friend who typically sees the world like you do. Look for—and be—the brother or sister who fears the Lord. You will be a reliable source of godly wisdom for each other.

Listening to advice and accepting discipline may be painful, which is why the word *sharpening* is apt, but both are essential to growing in wisdom. For example, this sharpening can be particularly helpful—and hard to submit to—in matters of dating and marriage. Single parents who are considering introducing children to a new love interest or remarrying need to seek counsel from prayerful friends who know all the personalities involved, including and maybe especially those of the children. When done wisely and well, the creation of stepfamilies can be redemptive for everyone, but it takes prayer, communication, counsel, and time.

Prayerful counsel works both ways. Married Christians: God may give your single friends a word of wisdom you need to hear about your marriage. Consider the counsel they offer. Along the same lines, your single-parent friends will likely understand some elements of parenting that you do not. Chances are, they have relied on God in the places where you have relied on your spouse. Do them the honor and do yourself the favor of asking your single friends for their marriage and parenting wisdom.

If we want to be counted among the wise, we must exercise honesty and humility in our community of believers. Sometimes that means we need to say things our friends don't want to hear or heed wisdom we don't much want to hear. Regarding Proverbs 27:17, Ray Ortlund says:

A real friend will provoke you and challenge you. You will not agree with everything your friend says, but you will want to listen. We all need that. Our various family backgrounds [and our current family structures!] left every one of us at least a little weird. So we need an honest friend from outside the tightly knit family to round us out. Every one of us needs to go to another person and say "Help me see myself. Help me get sharper for Christ."[3]

Sometimes the most valuable sharpening happens across gender lines. The church must be a place where men and women can safely develop Christ-centered friendships without fear of sparking temptation or creating opportunity for sin. I cannot overstate how crucial these friendships can be for single parents and their children. As a mother raising three sons, I relied heavily on several of the men in my church (including our pastor but by no means limited to him) for guidance and advice. I had never been a teenage boy, I didn't know what was "normal" and what was something to worry about, and I didn't know how to relate to my guys sometimes. My husband wouldn't have had all the answers either, but these men offered perspectives I needed. They reassured me and counseled me, and because they spent so much time getting to know my sons, they gave guidance to my boys too. I shudder to think where my boys and I would be right now without the friendship of the many Christian men who have loved us well.

These friendships should not be limited to single parents who are raising opposite-sex children like me. One single mom raising daughters openly shared how much she misses having men who are deeply invested in her daughters' lives. The absence of male presence and perspective has only added to their loss, and she worries that her daughters don't know what a godly man looks like. I spoke with a single dad who wishes his adopted son had more relationships with women who could bring a different kind of nurture into his life.

Male-female friendships in the church are admittedly complex and outside the scope of our discussion here, but if we want to support single parents well, such relationships are essential. More than one woman I interviewed described feeling as if people in the church—both men and women—found her "dangerous" or "threatening" after she became single again, which only led to more isolation. Certainly, every member of the church must commit to support the marriage vows and the holy sexuality of every other member in order for these friendships to be a blessing and not a curse. The pitfalls are real: in my interviews, I heard stories of elders and church leaders propositioning single mothers, making them objects of unwanted infatuations. But we must stop being afraid to form Christ-centered friendships across gender lines. Our view of the kingdom is incomplete without each other. Cultivating relationships in the church and in the world always brings dangers and temptations. But that should never stop us from pursuing the fullness of what God has for us in Christ-centered relationships with other people.

For our family, these friendships brought so much joy because in every case, if a husband was committed to my boys and to me, his wife was equally invested. Their whole family befriended our whole family. We became what Scripture calls *brothers and sisters*, across different ages and different genders, true family who can freely enjoy and care for one another as God intended.

The Rest of Paul's Story

Seeking wisdom about finding a church for his family, single father Paul prayed with James 1:5 in mind: "If any of you lacks wisdom, you should ask God, who gives generously to all without finding fault, and it will be given to you." God extends a warm invitation to ask for the wisdom we need. He will never blame or shame us for not knowing what we don't know. Nor will our Father be stingy with the insight and guidance we need; he is glad to give it. Whether you are raising kids alone or simply living as a finite human with a limited and imperfect point of view, approach God with both awe and assurance.

Paul asked for the guidance he needed, and God gave it. By God's grace, Paul found a church that feels like true family for him and his kids. Walking in the first few times wasn't any easier than it had been anywhere else, but he quickly realized that the people he met saw him as just a regular new guy. He could let his guard down because he never sensed judgment or even nosiness, only genuine warmth and a friendly "we're glad you're here" welcome. What impressed him even more was the way the church embraced his kids. They were welcome anywhere he went. Men and women of all ages showed sincere interest in getting to know him and his kids and inviting them into the fellowship of the church.

Paul attributes their warm welcome to the freedom of the gospel. Secure in the love and salvation of Christ, members of his church can be honest with their struggles because they know they will not be shamed but will be counseled and encouraged in God's truth. As a result, Paul sensed his new church home "fold his family in" when he finally shared their story. They have never been made to feel odd, and no one ever tries to "repair" him or his kids. Their church simply loves and cares for one another, difficulties and all, like the family God made them to be.

— *nine* —

God's Grace in Our Shame

Therefore, there is now no condemnation for those who are in Christ Jesus. (Romans 8:1)

I have not come to call the righteous, but sinners to repentance. (Luke 5:32)

I t took me years, and weekly talks with a good therapist, to accept that I am a person worth inviting somewhere."

Katherine and I sat in her kitchen while her youngest child played in the next room. As a twice-divorced mom of four, Katherine never left the church because, like the disciples, she didn't know where else to turn (John 6:68). But the heavy burden of shame has made belonging complicated.

Both of Katherine's husbands suffered from addiction. After her first husband threatened her with a knife, she did not hesitate to divorce him because she knew she had to keep her children safe. Feeling pressure to provide her first two children with a father drove her decision to marry a second time, but her second husband's troubles far exceeded the troubles of the first, as did the fallout from the second divorce.

For years she has felt the stigma of walking the halls of her church with a "D²" across her forehead (her expression for being twice divorced). She does not receive invitations to socialize or to join small group Bible studies. She feels that men don't want her to hang out with their wives (as if she might try to convince her girlfriends that singleness is better than marriage) and that women don't want her to talk to their husbands (as if a conversation would be the start of an affair). At times she wonders if people didn't want to see her or her children helped because she has brought her troubles on herself by being divorced twice. Pastors have been kind and helpful, but church members sometimes tend to avoid her. Sunday school teachers are quick to tell her how her children misbehave but offer little in the way of empathy or encouragement.

Understanding the Dynamics of Shame

According to Christian psychiatrist Curt Thompson, shame is "an undercurrent of sensed emotion" that persuades me to feel, and live out of, the sense that *I am not enough; There is something wrong with me; I am bad; or I don't matter.*[1] Shame convinces me that hope is futile, that I am "powerless to change [my] condition or circumstances. . . . *I do not have what it takes to tolerate this moment or circumstance.*"[2]

In the garden before the fall, Adam and Eve "were both naked, and they felt no shame" (Gen. 2:25). Their nakedness wasn't just literal. In their pure, sinless state, they had nothing to hide from each other or from God, who walked with them in the cool of the day. Comfortable in their own skin (and nothing else), Adam and Eve enjoyed a freedom and an intimacy that, millennia later, we can catch only in tantalizing glimpses. When we commune with God in prayer, when we lose ourselves in Spirit-filled worship, or when we stand before another human being with all our defenses down and feel the love in their gaze, we sense the faintest brush of the closeness we were meant for. We long to recapture these moments of knowing and being known, and yet being vulnerable terrifies us.

When the serpent questions Eve, he plants the very same doubts in her mind that shame still causes in us today. "Did God really say . . . ?" (Gen. 3:1) casts doubt on the character of God, as well as on her own ability to assess whether God is good. And if Eve cannot trust her discernment of God's goodness, she is deficient, lacking in wisdom. We know the challenge rattles Eve because she adds to God's directive that they not eat from the tree, saying that they also should not touch it (see Gen. 2:17; 3:3). The serpent then directly contradicts God's word, telling Eve that if she eats of the tree, she will not die, but rather her eyes will be opened and she will be "like God, knowing good and evil" (Gen. 3:5).

The implications of the serpent's questions are profound. In a brief exchange, he has suggested to Eve that she is *not enough.* To be enough, she needs to take matters into her own hands and eat the fruit. The serpent insinuates that because she does not know good and evil, there is *something wrong with her.* God is the one who made her, if not *bad,* then not as good as himself. The implication is that if she does not eat the fruit, then she *will not matter*—to God, to her husband, or to herself.

Believing it is up to her to go after what God failed to give her, needing to relieve this disruption to her peace of mind, Eve eats the fruit and shares with her willing husband.

God Encourages Us in Our Shame

According to shame researcher Brené Brown, two essential ingredients help to heal shame and restore connection: empathy and vulnerability.[3] Brown is simply naming what Jesus offers believers. For the healing of our relationships, first with himself and also with each other, God offers us perfect empathy and vulnerability in the person of Christ.

Empathy: Cared For by the Savior Who Feels Our Pain

Two verses from the book of Hebrews clearly demonstrate Jesus's empathic identification with fallen sinners. We will consider them together:

> We do not have a high priest who is unable to empathize with our weaknesses, but we have one who has been tempted in every way, just as we are—yet he did not sin. Let us then approach God's throne of grace with confidence, so that we may receive mercy and find grace to help us in our time of need. (Heb. 4:15–16)

> For this reason he had to be made like them, fully human in every way, in order that he might become a merciful and faithful high priest in service to God, and that he might make atonement for the sins of the people. Because he himself suffered when he was tempted, he is able to help those who are being tempted. (Heb. 2:17–18)

That truth that Jesus was willing to leave heaven and take on a mortal body, with all its discomforts and indignities; to subject himself to the rejection of men who were not worthy to lace his sandals; to accept his Father's turning away from him; to endure the weight of our sin—all this endears Jesus to me like nothing else. He did not have to endure any of it, but he chose it all for you and for me. What comfort we have knowing we can come to him without shame because *he knows*. Jesus has felt the weakness of human flesh. The creator of heaven and earth chose to identify himself with us and to suffer not only *for* us but also *with* us in the most personal way possible. His compassion overflows. We can trust him.

Vulnerability: Seen by the Father

When I visited a friend's church recently—her Christ-centered, Bible-believing, heart-for-the-hurting church—my friend remarked, "Yeah, we don't do vulnerability here."

By that she meant that members of her church carefully cultivate the appearance of the good and just as carefully cover up the bad and the ugly. As a result, they miss out on the closeness and healing that God intends his family to have in community.

Psalm 139 shows me that God already sees my heart and the thorny shame that I try to keep buried there.

> You have searched me, LORD,
>   and you know me.
> You know when I sit and when I rise;
>   you perceive my thoughts from afar.
> You discern my going out and my lying down;
>   you are familiar with all my ways.
> Before a word is on my tongue
>   you, LORD, know it completely.
> You hem me in behind and before,
>   and you lay your hand upon me.
> Such knowledge is too wonderful for me,
>   too lofty for me to attain. (vv. 1–6)

I wonder if I am the only one who reads these verses and feels exposed, guilty, and uncomfortable. Instead of finding God's familiarity "wonderful," does anyone else find his hand oppressive, his scrutiny frightening? When I read Psalm 139, I wonder if there is anywhere in the universe I can hide from the watchful eye of a God who reads my thoughts—thoughts that range from uncharitable to lewd to murderous—before I think them.

The psalmist wonders too:

> Where can I go from your Spirit?
>> Where can I flee from your presence?
> If I go up to the heavens, you are there;
>> if I make my bed in the depths, you are there.
> If I rise on the wings of the dawn,
>> if I settle on the far side of the sea,
> even there your hand will guide me,
>> your right hand will hold me fast. (vv. 7–10)

When failure or judgment (my own self-judgment or someone else's) has inflamed my shame, these verses feel like a threat. I can run, but I cannot hide.

However, when I read these verses through the lens of the death-defying, cross-bearing love of Christ for me, the same words feel very different. If I remember that Jesus lived his life determined to set me free from sin and death, that he died to give me his righteousness and rose again because I am, incredibly, the "joy set before him" (Heb. 12:2), what sounded like unbearable scrutiny is revealed to be devoted attention. He searches me not to criticize me but to sanctify me and make me into the image of Christ. He discerns the hardness of my heart and is not disappointed in me but determines to guide me and hold me and soften me to love. When I know the love of Christ is what holds me fast, the hand that weighed heavy feels warm, solid, steady, his grip on me both relentless and tender.

For the Katherines of the world—which is to say, for all of us who know the bitter taste of shame—these verses bring sweet relief.

> For you created my inmost being;
>> you knit me together in my mother's womb.
> I praise you because I am fearfully and wonderfully made;
>> your works are wonderful,
>> I know that full well.

My frame was not hidden from you
    when I was made in the secret place,
    when I was woven together in the depths of the earth.
Your eyes saw my unformed body;
    all the days ordained for me were written in your book
    before one of them came to be.
How precious to me are your thoughts, God!
    How vast is the sum of them!
Were I to count them,
    they would outnumber the grains of sand—
    when I awake, I am still with you. (Ps. 139:13–18)

Once I accept that God handcrafted me for exactly the days he ordained me to live—including the difficult days of raising children alone—and once I accept that God thinks I am wonderful, I don't have to be afraid of what God sees when he looks at me. Every moment of my existence has been lived in God's plain sight. Nothing about me surprises him, shocks him, disappoints him, or makes him regret me. Instead of cowering behind wilted fig-leaf defenses, I am free to throw myself wide open to him:

Search me, God, and know my heart;
    test me and know my anxious thoughts.
See if there is any offensive way in me,
    and lead me in the way everlasting. (vv. 23–24)

What This Means for the Church

Please understand: single parents are exceptionally vulnerable to shame. Drawing from Curt Thompson's teaching about the lies shame tells, imagine what shame might sound like in the private thoughts of the single mom or dad:

I am not enough . . . because my husband left me for that girl.

There is something wrong with me . . . because I never could make my wife happy.

I am bad . . . because I got pregnant when I wasn't married.

I don't matter . . . because she chose alcohol over me.

If we don't feel shame about our circumstances, we certainly do feel shame based on our limitations as a parent:

I am not enough . . . because I can't afford to pay for my child's winter coat.

There is something wrong with me . . . because I dread going to church.

I am bad . . . because I burden my oldest child with my worries about his little sister.

I don't matter . . . because if I did, someone would see that I am drowning.

As we've seen, in the single-parent life there is never enough time, attention, money, energy, or wisdom. We can't be in two places at once, and we don't have a money tree, and we don't know how to help our anxious child. Shame wants us to believe the lie that our felt inadequacy will harm our child, that in fact we're so deficient, there's not much we can do about any of it.

As Christians, we must ask ourselves how we might unintentionally compound the shame of the single parent. A new family visits church: only dad and two kids, no wedding ring. Do we need to know where the mom is and why she isn't there before we embrace our brother and his children? Say there's a mom in your office with a couple of divorces under her belt. Do you need to find out if those divorces had biblical grounds before you invite her to join your Bible study?

The apostle Paul has a word for how we should befriend single parents: "Those parts of the body that seem to be weaker are indispensable, and the parts that we think are less honorable we treat with special honor" (1 Cor. 12:22–23). This is not to say that single parents are "less honorable" or "unpresentable" (v. 23) in God's sight, only that their painful stories are often more visible to the public than the struggles that go on in other homes. A divorce is harder to hide than a contentious marriage, so it may *seem* that divorced folks or unmarried parents are, to use Paul's word, "weaker." But only God knows the true state of our hearts toward him. Remember Katherine, who refuses to quit church because she finds Jesus there, even with the D^2 on her forehead. Paul declares people like Katherine *indispensable*. They are crucial, nonnegotiable members of the body of Christ, and we are to treat them with *special honor*, not dishonor or neglect.

The Katherines in our congregations honor God when they go to church rather than skipping it because they are busy or tired, because the kids don't want to go, or because postpandemic, staying home is just easier. She has loved much because she is aware she has been forgiven much; he who has been forgiven little loves little (see Luke 7:36–50).

Writing about 1 Corinthians 12:22–23, Curt Thompson says,

> Here [Paul] casts a vision for a community of faith in which we carefully and diligently seek out, protect and honor those who are especially vulnerable and . . . whom we are easily tempted to be ashamed of, in the same way we are tempted to do the same with parts of each of our inner lives. We do this, as Jesus did with Peter in John [21:15–17], not only in order for them to be given the honor of forgiveness, healing, and protection, but also the commission to answer the vocational calling within the church which is uniquely theirs.[4]

Thompson calls our attention to Peter, whose denial of Jesus could easily have disqualified him from ministry or led him to hide forever in shame, especially given all his posturing before Jesus's arrest. Yet on the beach in John 21, Jesus honors the one who has been humiliated by reaffirming the calling on Peter's life to shepherd God's people. No longer confident in his own zeal, Peter will minister out of his new understanding of the grace he has received. The forgiveness Jesus offers him demolishes his need to defend himself or hide. His confidence is in Christ. Christ is the Rock that will hold; Peter's testimony of the grace of Jesus will stand.[5]

Honoring the Single Parent in Your Midst

We honor single parents because all members of Christ's body are called to "honor one another above yourselves" (Rom. 12:10). In Philippians, Paul gives us a more specific picture of what honoring someone looks like: "Do nothing out of selfish ambition or vain conceit. Rather, in humility value others above yourselves, not looking to your own interests but each of you to the interests of the others" (Phil. 2:3–4). In large part, that's what this book is about: examining ways we can put the interests of single parents and their children above our own.

But there's more to it. We honor single parents with special care and attention because raising children to love Jesus without the partnership of a spouse is hard. We honor them because they live at the end of their resources of time, money, energy, attention, and patience nearly every day, and yet they persevere. As it's been said, the dancer Ginger Rogers did everything her partner Fred Astaire did, only Ginger did it backward and in high heels. Single parents are dancing Fred's steps and Ginger's, and sometimes they do it gracefully. Single parents aren't looking for your admiration, but it sure would be a treat to receive your encouragement.

Like the apostle Peter, single parents who are intensely aware of their weakness and sin are also intensely aware of God's grace. As such, they have much to offer the body of Christ and a lot to teach you. Don't let shame build a wall between you and your sister or brother. Welcome single parents to your small group, Bible study, or Sunday school class. If that parent is inclined to share, listen and ask questions; if they are quiet, be sure to hang out and chat before or after. Be aware that they might have a hard time sitting in a room full of couples or listening to a group of moms bemoan their husbands' travel for work. (On that note, please never, ever say you are a single parent for the week because your spouse is out of town. Frankly, on a bad day you might make a single parent feel like punching you in the face. Even though your situation may reflect some aspects of single parenthood, it is insensitive to imply you know how it feels. Very few married parents have experienced what it is like for a single parent to bear the sole responsibility for their child, or to share that responsibility with an ex. Those whose spouses are deployed, seriously ill, or incarcerated have had a taste of it, but each of these is a special circumstance worthy of careful attention in the church.)

Be aware of single-parent families on Mother's Day and Father's Day.[6] If they come to church (our family tends to avoid church on Father's Day), it will probably be hard. Don't assume that all kids have a mother or a father. Some have neither. What would the Holy Spirit have you say to them? The parents need to know that you see them too. If you honor married parents, honor single ones too. Don't lump single mothers in with fathers on Father's Day, or commend fathers on Mother's Day. A mom cannot be a dad, and a dad cannot be a mom, and neither one could ever be both. To imply that they should be only adds to their load of impossible jobs.

When you see a single parent and their children in the pews, offer silent thanks to God. It may have been harder for them to get there than it was for you.

Overcoming Shame

Think back for a moment to Adam and Eve. They cover themselves with fig leaves *before* God approaches. They have already judged themselves, and so they anticipate that he will judge them too. The inner narrative of shame forces them into hiding before God ever confronts them, even though they know he is kind and loving. This is the predicament of any person struggling with shame—they preempt connection by hiding, even from people they know they can trust, because they don't feel good enough about themselves to be in relationship.

This is particularly relevant regarding Christians who have stopped attending church in the wake of a divorce or a loss. We shouldn't harass people who want to be left alone, but it's worth asking ourselves if we have let a brother or sister fall away because we felt too awkward to pursue them, or if we simply failed to notice them. We may also have neighbors and coworkers who were uncomfortable in whatever church they attended before or who have never been to church and aren't going to start now that they've become a single parent. Consider the possibility that shame or fear of judgment is part of that distance.

Of course, people can hide in the church too. They may attend services faithfully but never engage with anyone. Several single parents I interviewed view church as a "get in, get out" situation because they feel so self-conscious. A single parent may be physically present and even engaged but shares nothing of himself or herself in any meaningful way (this could be true for anyone in any stage of life). Real conversation and vulnerable sharing take work, and for those who are busy and tired, even chitchat can be exhausting. Consider how your church, and you personally, might remove obstacles to welcoming hurting people as individuals, each made in the image of God.

Finally, whether or not you are a single parent, each of us unmasks shame for the lies that it tells using the only antidote: the gospel. "God demonstrates his own love for us in this: While we were still sinners, Christ died for us" (Rom. 5:8). Even in your sinful state, Christ's love *made you enough* for him to give his life for you. In Christ there is nothing *wrong with you*; you are a new creation (2 Cor. 5:17). Looking at the cross, you can never say you *do not matter.* You matter infinitely to your heavenly Father.

Modeling Vulnerability

I will never forget the Sunday my pastor Jim Barnette visibly struggled in the middle of a sermon. Flustered and shaky, he asked first for a glass of water and then for a chair. He persevered through the sermon and left right after the service, promising that he was all right and would let us know if he needed anything.

The next few Sundays were business as usual. He thanked us for checking on him, assured us he had received medical attention, and moved right into his sermon. But about four weeks after that scary Sunday, he paused at the end of the service and said he needed to share something important.

Jim told us what had happened in the pulpit that Sunday was a panic attack. Mind you, the man had been a preaching minister and college professor—who taught preaching, no less!—for more than thirty years. He'd never had a panic attack, and the pulpit was the last place he ever would have expected anxiety to strike with such force. But what happened that Sunday led him to confront some parts of his life that he'd been avoiding and to make some changes that included keeping regular appointments with a counselor and taking better care of himself physically.

Jim felt his congregation needed to know the truth. Every time he climbed back into the pulpit, he feared that panic would set in again, that his weakness would show up in the very place where he once felt most confident. He was tempted to be ashamed of what happened, but he knew his weapon against that shame was to bring his fear into the light of the gospel and enlist his "tribe" (as he called us) to pray for him.

Jim's confession was simple, direct, and profound. Rather than hide, he exposed his own weakness, trusting that God wasn't ashamed of him and that we would be glad to care for him.

Our pastor modeled the courage and humility that come with being secure in Christ's love, a security that every believer can have if we will but trust him. Imagine what our churches could be if we offered each other a place to shed our coats of wilting fig leaves and slip on robes of Christ's glorious righteousness instead (Isa. 61:10).

Imagine if my friend could say of her church—if we all could say of our churches—"Yeah, we don't do shame here."

ten

Sin Separates Us, but the Gospel Makes Us Family

Therefore confess your sins to each other and pray for each other so that you may be healed. The prayer of a righteous person is powerful and effective. (James 5:16)

I am not good at asking for help," Lara says. "It's just much easier to do things for myself. I have gotten a little better at asking for help over the years, but I have also gotten better at just handling things on my own."

Lara's kids were still toddlers when her marriage ended because her husband's addictions were out of control. She divorced him and cut all ties to provide a stable home for her three children. If he can get clean, she is more than willing for her ex-husband to reengage with his kids, but over the past nine years he has been unable to stay off hard drugs.

In the first years after the divorce, when two of her children were still babies, Lara counted on her parents and siblings to offer support, advice, and extra pairs of hands. Church was a different story. A lifelong Catholic, Lara loves her church, but she keeps to herself when she attends. Even though her priest gave her unequivocal support for the divorce and continues to care for her, she is reluctant to engage with other parishioners because she is uncomfortable telling people she is divorced. Pride and fear of judgment keep her distant. Lara also finds spiritual support in Alcoholics Anonymous and in a local nondenominational church.

And still her inability to ask for help plagues her. She shakes her head. "It's pride. I know it's my pride. But still. If I can handle it, and I can, why would I ask for help?"

We need look no further than the tragic tale of Genesis 3 to explain why all our relationships are broken. Sin separates us from God and each other, and only through Jesus do we have any hope for reconciliation.

This chapter takes a different approach than the first nine. Chapters 1 through 9 focused on particular challenges of unmarried parents and how the church might come alongside these families in love. In this chapter we will examine the ways in which sin, which affects every believer, divides us from each other so that we cannot give or receive love from one another as God intends. We will first look at the sins that tempt single parents, and then we'll examine the sins that can prevent other Christians from loving single-parent families well.

Some parts of this chapter may sound harsh. I use the word *sin* intentionally because that is what it is. We all need a wake-up call to the ways we fall short of loving each other. I was once a single adult, I was a married parent for thirteen years, and I have been a single parent for thirteen years. I know these sins because I have committed them (and still do). If we don't call sin what it is, we stay stuck in it. By the grace of God, he convicts us and the Holy Spirit makes repentance and change possible. May we be stirred to compassion for each other's struggles and to the confession and repentance of our own.

Temptations for Single Parents

The hard truth for single parents is that some days we can be our own worst enemies.

I am not talking about the ways we may have contributed to our current status as a single mom or dad, although our failures to love wisely or well have long-term effects on everyone in the family. (The same is true for single people and married parents.) Single parents face particular temptations that arise from how we think about our single parenthood. We can be easy prey for pride, self-pity, envy, and bitterness. If we give in and let these rule us, we teach our children to live out the same sinful patterns. What's more, our sin hurts our kids by isolating our family from people who might be able to help us, preventing our kids from getting the very love and nurture we want them to have. Indulging these sins prevents other Christians from truly knowing our families. Relationships can't grow if we wrap ourselves in a cloak of stand-offish independence. Onetime single mother Vaneetha Rendall Risner writes, "One of the cruelest things Satan does in our suffering is persuading us that we don't need to be rescued from him, but rather to be understood, revered, and left alone."[1]

Self-Pity

For a classic portrait of self-pity, picture the prophet Jonah, sitting dejected under his wilted plant outside the city of Nineveh.

Jonah did not want to preach to the Ninevites, so he boarded a ship headed in the opposite direction. He wound up saved by the miraculous provision of a whale, and his belated obedience led to a great repentance across the entire city.

But Jonah never liked the Ninevites, he didn't want them to be saved, and he doesn't appreciate being the vehicle of their deliverance. He's so angry about his success that he wants to die (Jonah 4:3). Then his plant wilts and he's left to wallow in the broiling hot sun, which makes him want to die all over again (v. 9). Full of self-righteous indignation, Jonah is mad because he feels the Ninevites don't deserve God's mercy and he doesn't deserve to be hot. (The shade thing would be hilarious except that I recognize myself throwing a pity party over something dumb.) Forgetting that he does not deserve God's mercy either, Jonah takes Nineveh's reprieve as a personal affront.

Self-pity endangers contentment and gratitude by convincing single parents that, as Jonah believed, God has done us wrong. Self-pity rejects the circumstances of our lives and declares them "not good enough for me." What's more, self-pity can lead us to justify other sins. "I deserve to have some fun," we think as we indulge in online shopping we can't afford. "That jerk doesn't deserve a second chance at marriage," we think when our ex announces his engagement. "My ex-wife deserves for me to tell our kids what she did." All the while, we believe that we—not to mention our kids!—deserve better than the single-parent life God has allowed for us, and we feel very sorry for ourselves indeed.

Our children are perceptive. They will know if we think we have earned better than what we have in our life with them. Being a single parent is undeniably difficult, but we never want our kids to feel as if they are the cause of those difficulties. If they sense our unhappiness with our situation, they won't be able to feel our love.

Bitterness and Envy

One spring I laid new sod in my backyard. Keeping it healthy felt like a full-time job. By nature, weeds took over, choking the slower-growing, prettier grass. I had a routine of diligent daily weeding: in the cool of the morning, I gently pulled the seedlings by hand, taking care to get the roots. In the afternoon, I watered the sod to soften the ground for the next morning's work. Otherwise, the ground would be too hard and the roots wouldn't give easily.

The root of bitterness is as tough as crabgrass. Hebrews 12:15 warns us to "see to it that no one falls short of the grace of God and that no bitter root grows up to cause trouble and defile many." The seeds of bitterness fall frequently: unfair circumstances and unkind people sow envy, resentment, self-pity, and unforgiveness in our hearts and minds, causing trouble and stirring up sin in everyone around us.

Cain kills Abel in a jealous rage because he thinks God prefers Abel. Resentment consumes Joseph's brothers, and they sell him into slavery and allow their father to think he is dead. Naomi loses her husband and two sons and asks to be called Mara, meaning "bitter," because grief has destroyed her hope for the future. Yearning for David's popularity literally drives Saul mad. The Pharisees deliver Jesus to be crucified out of envy (Matt. 27:18 ESV). When bitterness grows unchecked, it destroys lives. Uprooting those seeds takes vigilance.

The whole Bible tells what God has done to reconcile us to himself, but the story of the reunion between Jacob and Esau is particularly beautiful. As boys, these two brothers clash because their parents play favorites. With help from his mom, Jacob tricks his brother out of his birthright and steals Esau's blessing, then runs for his life because Esau wants to kill him. Years later, God speaks to Jacob in a dream and tells him to return home. Jacob obeys, but he is terrified at the thought of meeting Esau, whom he wronged so badly. Jacob sends extravagant gifts ahead to appease his brother and even travels behind his enormous family so that he can gauge his big brother's mood before he has to confront him.

To Jacob's surprise and delight, Esau runs to meet him and grabs him in a tearful hug. All is forgiven; all that is left is brotherly love. Esau asks Jacob why he sent gifts ahead; Jacob replies that he was trying to "find favor" with his brother. Esau's response is beautiful: "*I have enough*, my brother; keep what you have for yourself" (Gen. 33:9 ESV, italics mine).

How could Esau forgive such deep betrayal? The key lies in those three little words: "I have enough." Bitterness says, "I have been treated poorly." Contentment says, "I have enough." Envy says, "What that person has is better than what I have." Peace says, "I have enough." Bitterness says, "Someone will pay for what has happened to me." Forgiveness says, "I have enough." Envy says, "No one else suffers like I do." Satisfaction says, "I have enough."

Like weeding new sod, pulling out bitterness and envy takes a lot of work. We have to fight to believe that in Christ we have enough and in him we are enough. Jesus tells us that "the work of God is this: to believe in the one he has sent" (John 6:29). We work to believe that God's "divine power" has given us "*all things* that pertain to life and godliness" (2 Peter 1:3 ESV, italics mine). We work to believe that he is working *all things* together for our family's good (Rom. 8:28). By doing the work of believing, we train our hearts to be content with the life God has given us. When we truly believe we have enough, we open our hearts wide in love and walk in the freedom Christ died to give us (Gal. 5:1).

Temptations for Singles and Married Parents

Before I became a single mom, I didn't notice the single parents around me much. It never occurred to me that their lives might be significantly more complicated than mine, nor did I wonder why I met single parents at my kids' schools but didn't meet them at church. If I am brutally honest, I felt pity for the single mom whose children were late to everything, but I didn't offer to help her carpool. Nor did I want my son to spend the night at his friend's dad's house, because I worried that a single dad might let the kids watch inappropriate movies.

God help me, I was so smug, and I didn't even know it.

Pride and Judgment

Those who don't get pregnant before marriage or who manage to stay married rather than divorce can be tempted to think they have done things "right." Even though we might never say it out loud or in so many words, this belief implies that the divorced person has done something wrong and we have not. Likewise, we might not be blunt and call their actions sin, but we slyly refer to pregnant unmarried moms as having "done things out of order." We wear our celibate singleness or married bliss like a churchy status symbol, proof that we are living life as God intended, while that single parent, unless widowed, clearly has sinned along the way.

One pastor's wife acknowledged that before she lost her husband, she looked at the single parents in their pews and assumed that bad choices or irresponsibility contributed to their circumstances. Perhaps the divorced parent had not "counted the cost" for their child before they left the marriage. She had scarcely registered her judgment when she wondered if maybe single parents didn't quite love their children enough, until she found herself in their shoes.[2] I appreciate her honesty. I have been guilty of the same judgments.

If you are married, you have not so much "done things right"—as you have been blessed with a gift. You sin in your marriage, yet by God's grace, you are still married. If you are single, you have not been blameless in every aspect of your singlehood. In either case, if you are pursuing holiness and loving others well, God through his Spirit enables your obedience and sustains you in your war against personal sin. Thank him for it! But don't take your blessings or your repentance as occasion for pride. You don't know the intimate details of that single parent's story, and even if you did, you cannot see what God sees when he looks at that person. Such things are none of your business. Your business is to love that person and their child well.

No matter how they came to be a single parent, that dad or mom is a sinner just like you. Just like me. They need Jesus, just like you, just like me. Don't let judgment divide you from that family. You have much to offer each other.

Busyness

As I said earlier, I didn't know what single parents struggled with, nor did I try to find out. On the one hand, it makes sense. We wear busyness as a badge of honor in modern-day America. Each of us has our own jobs, responsibilities, and people to care for.

But even in church, we are tempted to seek out what my friend jokingly calls "PLUs"—people like us—and stick to doing our service projects and mission trips with the people we already like and feel comfortable with. There are some good reasons for developing small groups with people of the same age or in the same stage. Commiserating over aging bodies or the early days of parenthood has its place because we all need to know we are not alone. But consider whether anyone is providing this kind of community for the single dad in your midst. Which Sunday school class is a fit for him? Your church may have several single moms, but if you silo them into a class of women just like them, how will they befriend the single and married men and women? If you do offer classes for single moms or single dads, are they led by married people, or by single adults?

If you make time for PLUs, you can also make a place in your life for people who aren't so much like you. Cliques are so middle school. There is no place for them in the church.

Modern Americans tend to overcommit, and parsing priorities can be complicated. But Jesus tells us the first and greatest commandment, paired with its corollary: Love God with all your heart, soul, and mind, and love your neighbor as yourself (Matt. 22:37–39). Genuine love is nothing if not time-consuming, demanding that we slow down, pray, pay attention, listen for the Spirit, and be present with people. When we stay wrapped up in our personal comfort zones or move too fast to truly see the people around us, we cannot love others well.

Apathy

"If anyone has material possessions and sees a brother or sister in need but has no pity on them, how can the love of God be in that person? Dear children, let us not love with words or speech but with actions and in truth" (1 John 3:17–19).

The apostle John tells us that love is compassion expressed in action and truth. If we feel genuine concern for the single-parent families in our church, we will do something about it. Love does not sit back on its heels and simply feel sorry for people; love prays and then acts in obedience to the Holy Spirit.

Church is not the place to put up our feet and make ourselves comfortable. If we are there to check a box, to project an image of being a "good person," or to make ourselves feel good about ourselves, we've missed the point (and the gospel) entirely. The gospel confronts us with our sin, our need for a Savior, and the grace of God, thereby banishing apathy for good. If we don't let these truths humble us and fill us with love for God and neighbor every time we walk in the door, then we are just going through some Christian motions.

What Church Family Looks Like

All families are broken by sin. As much as we like to post "one big happy family" photos on social media, none of us live in a household that is as pretty as we'd like to project. Yet many of us share vague ideals of what family *could* look like, ideals that in the absence of a marriage exist permanently out of reach.

In our best imaginings, families live, work, play, and eat together and clean up each other's messes. Much to the chagrin of small children, they share. Members of a family ally themselves in a harsh world, looking out for each other. Resemblance goes beyond big noses, red hair, or a common aptitude for singing; members of a family often share habits, convictions, preferences, and quirks. Inside jokes, favorite recipes, and common enemies bind them together, though everyone will remember the stories a little differently. Most of all, though, family ties commit us to the well-being of the others, often at the expense of self. Each person belongs to all the others in the family, dedicated to each other's good and to the good of the family. Come what may, in an ideal family you cannot lose your belonging any more than you can lose your family's love.

Believers in Christ belong to that type of family. Membership is both more wonderful and more challenging than we can imagine.

The Holy Spirit testifies to all believers that they have become children of God, adopted into his family so that we, like Jesus, may call on him as our Father (Rom. 8:14–17). That adoption brings us into a new and glorious union with our Maker and Creator, but it also brings us into a wholly new relationship with each other. This corporate dimension of our adoption demands our attention because no matter how much or how little we have in common on the surface, those who are in Christ share the Spirit of God. Fellow believers become brothers and sisters. God's family even takes precedence over human family (Matt. 12:46–50). While this is never an excuse to abandon our biological connections (Jesus provided for his mother from the cross, John 19:26–27), the magnitude of the family of God offers us deeper belonging than any nuclear family ever could. Unbound by time, geography, race or ethnicity, status, ability, language, or any human construct, God's family is our true and eternal family. The local church is the temporal expression of that family, which means the local church is utterly essential in the life of a Christian.

What This Means for the Church

Just as a child newly born or adopted into a family receives nurture and learns to be a member of that household, the local church is where we give and receive what we need to grow as members of God's household (Eph. 2:19). The Bible characterizes this family in the following ways:

Commitment—We are so invested in each other that we lay down our lives for one another (1 John 3:16).

Family resemblance—In Christ, our "new selves" are "created to be like God in true righteousness and holiness" (Eph. 4:24).

Unity—In the upper room Jesus prayed that we may be brought to complete unity, and we know his prayer will be answered (John 17:23).

Diversity—God's family encompasses people from every nation, tribe, people, and language from across the world (Rev. 7:9).

Inseparability—God's family is one body, one temple, members one of another, joined by one Spirit, with faith in one Father (Rom. 12:5).

Sharing—Each one of us has been given gifts for the benefit of the whole family of God (1 Peter 4:10).

Servanthood—Jesus set the example when he washed his disciples' feet; we do the same for one another (John 13:14).

Confession—Our church family is a safe, compassionate place to confess sin and receive prayer for healing (James 5:16).

Restoration—The Spirit leads brothers and sisters to gently restore anyone who is caught in sin (Gal. 6:1).

Provision—God's grace can work so powerfully among us that there is no needy family in our church (Acts 4:34).

Work—Because we are co-laborers with Christ, we are co-laborers with each other (1 Cor. 3:9).

Burden-bearing—We don't leave each other to struggle alone under difficulties and responsibilities, but we share in each other's burdens (Gal. 6:2).

Encouragement—We encourage each other and build each other up (1 Thess. 5:11).

Feeling—Our hearts are so entwined that we rejoice for and with each other, and we mourn for and with each other (Rom. 12:15).

Togetherness—Meeting together regularly and frequently is an essential part of loving and encouraging each other (Heb. 10:24–25).

Love—To love one another is to live in the light (1 John 2:10). In the household of God, love "always protects, always trusts, always hopes, always perseveres" (1 Cor. 13:7).

All that sounds so wonderful, doesn't it? But all the things that make biological family complicated can make church family complicated too. We don't pick our biological (or adoptive) moms, dads, or siblings, and we don't pick the folks in our local church. (Given a choice, they might not pick me either.) Because every member of that church is a sinner in need of grace, you will cause each other a lot of trouble. Your church family will annoy you, frustrate you, undermine you, leave you out, and hurt your feelings. You will fail them, let them down, talk behind their backs, ignore their suffering, and wear them out. That is what life in any family is like, so we can't be surprised when sin separates us.

Let's ask God to reveal the ways in which our hearts are hard toward each other, where we are so self-involved that we cannot see other people clearly. Rather than allowing "church as family" to become a meaningless cliché, let's carefully examine what God intends for us to mean to each other and how that plays out in both word and action. After all, God makes us family to teach us to love like he loves.

The Love of God Binds *Every* Family Together

In Ephesians 3:14–21, praying for believers, Paul directs our attention to our Father, whose paternal claim on *every* family in heaven and on earth is what makes us brothers and sisters. Every *you* in the prayer is plural. Every one of the blessings he prays for, we receive together. We are strengthened in the power of the Spirit together. Christ lives in our hearts through faith together. God will grow our roots down into love because it's going to take *all of us together* to grasp the glory of the love of Christ. We can only know that love together. And then, together, God will fill us to overflowing with his fullness.

Having loving unity in the body of Christ may seem like a dream, a wish, and a prayer, but God promises he can do the impossible.

> For this reason I kneel before the Father, from whom every family in heaven and on earth derives its name. I pray that out of his glorious riches he may strengthen you with power through his Spirit in your inner being, so that Christ may dwell in your hearts through faith. And I pray that you, being rooted and established in love, may have power, together with all the Lord's holy people, to grasp how wide and long and high and deep is the love of Christ, and to know this love that surpasses

knowledge—that you may be filled to the measure of all the fullness of God.

Now to him who is able to do immeasurably more than all we ask or imagine, according to his power that is at work within us, to him be glory in the church and in Christ Jesus throughout all generations, for ever and ever! Amen. (Eph. 3:14–21)

— *eleven* —

God's Grace Is Sufficient for Every Family

He said to me, "My grace is sufficient for you, for my power is made perfect in weakness." Therefore I will boast all the more gladly about my weaknesses, so that Christ's power may rest on me. That is why, for Christ's sake, I delight in weaknesses, in insults, in hardships, in persecutions, in difficulties. For when I am weak, then I am strong. (2 Corinthians 12:9–10)

When my kids were little, we sang a song about going on a bear hunt. In each verse the intrepid bear hunters encounter obstacles, like a patch of grass or a cave. To stay on the hunt, they have to deal with the problem in front of them:

> Can't go over it,
> Can't go under it,
> Can't go around it,
> Got to go through it . . .

That's not a bad way to describe what being a parent feels like. Every day presents its challenges—some days, more like insurmountable obstacles—and we aren't sure how we will get our children through to the other side. But we know there is no way around it. Christian parents dream of raising their children in love and faith and the joy of the Lord, nurturing their relationships and their gifts and keeping them safe and healthy, but these things are very, very hard to do, whether you're married or not. Every parent has to "go through it," but the single parent goes through it alone, knowing their family won't make it without help.

Therein lies the great gift of parenting alone: we are well acquainted with our weaknesses. We know we are not enough. The single-parent life strips away any illusion that "you've got this!" or "you're *killing* it" (feels more like it is killing you). We confront our not-enoughness before we open our eyes in the morning. Fear, grief, exhaustion, and loneliness dog our days, clouding our minds and draining our strength. We need more: no lone parent can offer enough protection, provision, and wisdom to meet their child's needs. Shame turns us in on ourselves and cuts us off from fellowship so that sin takes advantage of our vulnerability and makes us doubt the goodness of God toward our families.

God invites us to embrace our weakness, for in it, we find that he is more than enough.

God's Grace Is Enough for Your Family

Let's look back to where we started: with the God who sees the single parent and their child. Recall Hagar in the desert with Ishmael, exposed and alone, with no one coming to help. She has done nothing to deserve or earn God's attention, yet he sets his love on her and her child (Deut. 7:7). God comes looking for them in order to bless them, and he is doing the same for you. God's gaze is intimate; his commitment is steadfast; his care is compassionate. He knows your past, your present, and your future, which looks so different from what you had hoped. He sees your every heartache and your every need. His loving care encompasses your child too. Though Genesis doesn't use the word, we recognize what God gives Hagar and her boy: grace.

God's grace bookends everything we have examined in these pages. We started with God's gracious care for Hagar, and we're going to end with the sufficiency of God's grace here. If you remember only one thing from reading this book, I want you to remember that God's grace is enough for your family. I know this because my sons and I have lived it. I have seen it in the lives of other single-parent families. But don't believe it because I say it's true—believe it because God's Word says it is so.

Paul writes to the Corinthians about an experience he had being "caught up to the third heaven" (2 Cor. 12:2). What he saw there was beyond telling, so God gave him an undefined "thorn in [his] flesh" to keep Paul from becoming "conceited" about his glimpse of paradise (v. 7). That thorn torments him such that he begs God to remove it three times, but God tells Paul that his grace is enough:

> He said to me, "My grace is sufficient for you, for my power is made perfect in weakness." Therefore I will boast all the more gladly about my weaknesses, so that Christ's power may rest on me. That is why, for Christ's sake, I delight in weaknesses, in insults, in hardships, in persecutions, in difficulties. For when I am weak, then I am strong. (2 Cor. 12:9–10)

God does not remove the thorn. He does not change Paul's circumstance or make his struggle any easier. He does not give Paul what he wants or what he thinks he needs. And yet Paul's experience of God's grace is so satisfying that he prefers the weakness the thorn causes him to his former, pre-thorn strength. Paul *boasts* and *delights* in whatever difficulties God allows, not because he is a masochist but because the strength of God he experiences in his weakness fulfills him more than being free of suffering would. In this way, the thorn itself is transformed into a grace, a gift reminding Paul that his own efforts to save himself or obey God will never be enough. The weaker he is, the more he relies on God's strength. And God is very strong indeed.

Our children are not thorns, but parenting them on our own is. And sometimes that thorn digs so deep you cry out for relief. It will not be removed, nor would you want it to be.

It is hard to accept that some of our family's needs will appear to go unmet. You may not have the money you need to pay your bills. You may not get the court order that would keep your child safe from an ex you don't trust. You may endure the rebellion of a beloved daughter without support from her other parent. It is right to lament all that you do not understand, to plead with the Father who sees you and your children. Circumstances may threaten to strangle your hope and crush your will beyond enduring, but your weakness is the very place where God's power is made perfect.

Paradoxically, if we believe Paul, we can be glad in the middle of pain and difficulty because of the sweetness of the grace we find there. You can do things in God's strength that you could never do in your own.

The sufficiency of God's grace is as mysterious as it is real, and I confess that I struggle to find words to explain what our family's experience has been. Time and again I have fallen to my knees, overwhelmed by the struggles we have faced together. I have despaired in the face of unanswered questions and deeply ingrained sin. Rarely has God given quick or neat resolutions. Parched for wisdom, disabled by fear, desperate with need, lonely beyond enduring, I have been overcome with weakness and have nearly lost hope.

And yet.

God is the lifter of my head (Ps. 3:3). His mercies truly are new every morning (Lam. 3:22–23). He keeps filling my lungs with air. The sun rises every day. Clouds and storms may obscure it; the light may be dim indeed, but it is there, and it always will be. He doesn't have to do these things for us. He set his affection on us because he loves us (Deut. 7:7–8). We find irrefutable proof of that love in the cross of Christ, the fullest expression of God's grace.

By grace we have been saved through the willing death of Jesus (Eph. 2:8). For our sakes he submitted himself to the limitations of being human, the helplessness of being nailed to a cross, and the prison of a lifeless body. In that weakness God displayed the strength that overcame death. We are children of the God who is stronger than death, and he uses that strength to rescue us from sin and its consequences. By his grace, resurrection is what God does. Our weakness is not an obstacle for him. He will accomplish his good work on our behalf.

In the life, death, and resurrection of Jesus, God's grace secured for us all that we ever truly need.

But God, too, is a parent, a Father who delights to give "every good and perfect gift" to his children (James 1:17). God's grace provides abundantly for the here and now too. "So do not worry, saying, 'What shall we eat?' or 'What shall we drink?' or 'What shall we wear?' For the pagans run after all these things, and your heavenly Father knows that you need them" (Matt. 6:31–32). Our weakness reminds us that he is the one who puts food on the table and gas in the car, who provides for co-pays and eyeglasses, often through the generous hands of our brothers and sisters. Our weakness reminds us that God is sanctifying us in community with our church and our children, making us more patient and less selfish. Our weakness reminds us to pray first, to follow him instead of figuring it out on our own, to trust instead of trying to fix everything, to ask for help instead of soldiering on alone. His strength sustains us to endure what we think might kill us and transforms us into women and men full of long-suffering love for our children and for his church. His strength makes us into generous givers of the grace we have received. His strength is the power that raised Christ from the dead (Eph. 1:19–20). We need not fear that his strength will fail.

God graciously meets our needs in a million ways, large and small, but this is a promise you can build your family on: God's grace is enough.

What This Means for the Church

Come close enough to know us, brothers and sisters, and what you see God doing in our families will astound you. He has given us a testimony of his strength in our weakness, and he will give you one in yours. Just listen to some of our voices:

> God gives me his grace every day when I wake up. I would never wish my situation on anyone, and some days I wake up questioning God and very angry. But I continue to pray for redemption, peace, salvation, courage . . . and every day when I wake up, he continues to give me that strength and grace. I have survived all my worst days because of him, and he will continue to sustain me.

> I have so many instances of God's grace in my family's life. My kids and I have always had a place to live, a car to drive, food, etc. The truth is, many times God intervened in spite of me to provide.

> Through my journey as a single parent, I have learned that I have to renew my reliance on the Lord every single moment. Every morning I remind myself not to focus on the future or all the scary things outside my control, but rather to sit and realize I am not alone but yoked with Jesus.

I have certainly seen God's grace in the way that the community (church, neighborhood, friends, etc.) have rallied around my child and me. Whether the neighbor down the street stops by to clean the gutters, fix the mailbox, or shovel the driveway when it snows, knowing that someone is looking out for our safety and comfort and taking it upon themselves to do the chores that might be challenging for me is a clear demonstration of God's grace and loving our neighbors.

Raising my child alone was hard because of all the medical issues. He went through so many surgeries, speech therapy, and special education that I had to fight professionals to provide for him. I knew that every step of the way people were praying for him and our family. On every occasion, God has shown up for us. My church family has covered me and my transgressions from having an outspoken, active mouth. Our church has provided financially so many times. My kids have been blessed with so many opportunities. People who didn't even know we needed it have poured into our lives. My son is grown now. He is not bitter or jaded from everything he went through. He is an honorable, hardworking man of God. He is a gifted prayer warrior. I continue to trust God even though I struggle to trust others. We as a family offer grace to others because that has been the example set for us.

This side of heaven, all families are broken by sin and death. Regardless of marital status or the presence (or absence) of children, every family needs God's grace. What God has done, is doing, and will do in our single-parent family, he can do in yours. Become part of our story and let us become part of yours.

The adoption we enjoy in Christ Jesus has made us true family, brothers and sisters by the Spirit of God, "so in Christ we, though many, form one body, and each member belongs to all the others" (Rom. 12:5). Married or single, young or old, we belong to each other. As fellow citizens of God's kingdom, we share allegiance to a heavenly home. As members of God's household, we share bonds that go way deeper than DNA. Built like a house on the foundation of Christ, we will someday fit together snugly (Eph. 2:19–20). Construction is still underway: "You too *are being built together* to become a dwelling in which God lives by his Spirit" (2:22, italics mine). God leaves no believer out as he crafts his home, so we shouldn't either. You cannot grow into the fullness God has for you without me, and I cannot grow without you. This family of God is itself a grace. May we embrace one another in the love of our Father, which never fails.

God's Grace to Daniel and His Son

Daniel lay awake most of the night staring at the ceiling, listening to the soft, shallow breathing of the tiny boy in the hotel crib. After years of pursuing international adoption, he was finally bringing his son home. Never married, Daniel felt God had called him to father an orphan, but all the prayer and planning had come down to this: one sleepless night, thousands of miles from home, wondering what he had been thinking to adopt a toddler on his own.

As dawn peeked over thick hotel curtains, exhaustion overtook Daniel and he fell asleep. Sometime later, the sweet sound of singing called him awake. He opened his eyes to a room lit with sunlight and the sight of his little boy sitting up in his crib, singing. He did not know the words or the tune—they did not even speak the same language yet—but the boy's bashful smile told his new father that all was well. God's grace bathed their family in love, and that grace was, and always has been, more than enough.

Single Parented

Our Story from One Son's Perspective

MAC HARRIS

> *Fear not, for I am with you;*
> *be not dismayed, for I am your God;*
> *I will strengthen you, I will help you,*
> *I will uphold you with my righteous right hand.*
> *(Isaiah 41:10 ESV)*

What do your parents do for work?"

It's a harmless question, really, and always asked with good intentions.

"Well, um, my dad was a lawyer, and my mom used to teach but now works for a ministry."

"Oh yeah? He was a lawyer? What does your dad do now?"

"Well, uh . . ."

I could never find the perfect answer to my least favorite question. It's not that I didn't want to admit the truth, but telling someone who didn't know me that my dad had *died* felt like reopening the scars on my elbows built up from a lifetime of sliding headfirst into second base. Sometimes I'd rush through my answer or mumble the past tense "was" or talk a lot about my mom's job to distract attention away from my dad. I'd do anything to defuse the situation and avoid making things awkward by dropping *that* bomb in an innocent conversation.

There are probably a dozen reasons why this conversation topic made me want to run and hide—I didn't want to be different, I didn't want someone else's pity, and I didn't want to be reminded of what I didn't want to think about, to name a few—but my internal struggle reflected a broader effort to minimize the reality that my dad's death was, to put it eloquently, a big deal.

Of course, everyone's story is unique, and my experience is by no means the norm for growing up in a single-parent house. Even my brothers probably reflect on our childhood differently (but then again, that's what brothers do). For some kids, the loss of a parent practically dominates all emotions and interactions; for others, it barely seems to register on the outside. But no matter the situation and no matter the story, growing up in a single-parent family is *always a really big deal*. It's an inescapable weight, grief, and differentness that no child or teenager (or adult, for that matter) should have to carry.

Still, no matter how many times someone would tell me, "This isn't something a thirteen-year-old should have to go through," I refused to admit that the loss affected me. I wanted to retreat inside myself, avoid emotional turmoil, and put up a good front for the outside world to see. And yet even though I didn't want help—from my mom, from my friends, from other parents, or from the God who had let this happen—the Father of the fatherless and protector of widows helped us every day (Ps. 68:5).

Relational Insurance

Last spring, I read an article by Jonathan Tjarks titled "Does My Son Know You?" If you haven't read the article, put this book down, go read it online, cry, and then come back when you're ready. Tjarks was a popular NBA writer and podcaster, and even though he worked for a large pop culture media company, he'd openly spoken about his faith on several occasions. (He also had a blog that was part NBA commentary, part Isaiah commentary. Does it get better than that?) This article, however, was different: Tjarks was nearly a year into a battle with terminal cancer, and his two-year-old-son would likely have to grow up without a dad.

For Tjarks, this was a particularly cruel blow—when he was six, his own dad was diagnosed with Parkinson's. He remembered shaking hands with all his dad's friends at his funeral and thinking, "I don't know any of you." He writes, "People talk a lot about medical insurance and life insurance when you get sick. But relational insurance is far more important. I didn't need my dad's money, but I could have used some of his friends."[1]

By the grace of God, this wasn't our experience. While you can't exactly "buy" relational insurance, my dad's friends (both husbands and their wives) have never stopped caring for us. Though we aren't their biological children, we are known and loved as if we were. As a teenage boy, I wanted to resist and push back. I didn't want help or pity or someone to treat me special. I didn't need to be babied, but I did need the love of a father.

And while no one person could replace my dad, God loved me with the love of a father through many other dads. No one tried to be my dad; they just cared, were curious, and kept showing up. In the midst of tragedy, God lavished his love on us through the care and dedication of many persistent people—both old friends and new. From season to season, the specifics would change, but there are too many people to thank for keeping our family afloat.

Help looked different in the stages of sickness, death, and the years that followed, and there is no single formula for anyone to follow. Some friends helped us buy a car or set aside money for college or assisted with plans for a different financial future.

Others helped out with braces, gave us summer jobs, offered baseball lessons, or came over to fix the toilet. Tickets to a cool game, a trip to a lake house, or an invite to the pool let us kids just be kids. Maybe it was taking us shopping for my mom's birthday or staying with us to give my mom a weekend away with her friends. A simple invite to grill out with another family meant so much because it let us feel like a normal family again for a night.

People stepped in for big and little things: to teach us how to shave or drive or deal with a breakup. Others wouldn't let us be strangers when we attended a new church.

But it was the consistent acts of kindness that stick out most. For years, other families brought us meals (which was more than fine by us), and we had rides to and from our practices. (This didn't just help my mom logistically but meant we got extra time with friends and quality time with other adults.) Years later, it's the letter every Christmas, the round of golf every time I'm in my hometown, the barbecue lunches, the weekly breakfast, the texts on Father's Day, and much more that still mean the world. These men aren't only father figures anymore, they are also my friends.

Of course, not everyone needs to be (or can be) the consistent presence in the lives of a single-parent family. Raising your own kids and caring for your own spouse are your *primary* calling (1 Tim. 5:8)—and no matter how challenging it is to raise kids as a single parent, it is *still* hard to raise kids with two parents! On top of that, I'll be the first to confess that kids who have dealt with divorce or death or abuse aren't always fun to be around. To care for the widow and the orphan requires sacrifice, and I'm so grateful to all the families who were willing to sacrifice a family meal to invite us in or take us out to dinner.

There are no quick solutions. There are no magic words to say or gifts to give or number of meals that will "fix" a grieving child, just as there's no formula for parenting *any* kid. But it's the consistent presence, the person who patiently builds the relational capital over years and years, who will change the life of a grieving kid. The person who's willing, like God, to draw near to the brokenhearted and ask the heavier questions that other people are afraid to ask (Ps. 34:18). The person who's willing to be stonewalled over and over again until we're ready to talk.

Sometimes that person had also grown up in a single-parent family and they knew I needed to be able to ask a man questions I didn't want to ask my mom. But often there wasn't anything special about *how* they came into our lives, it was simply that they were there. My dad was gone, but I still needed someone to show me what it looked like to be a friend, a husband, a father, and a man of God. Jeff was gone, but Jody, Sparty, Walter, Tom, Price, both Andys, both Gregs, and many others were right there.

Terrible, Tender Timing

God's grace in my family's tragedy goes beyond just the people he put in our lives. God's timing is often frustrating, but it is never accidental. Even in the shock of that cancer diagnosis, God was kind.

When my dad called my mom to tell her his diagnosis, she was on the interstate, driving from Birmingham to Charlotte to put a deposit down on our new rental house. We were days away from moving to North Carolina for my dad's new job. Had he visited the doctor a week later, we would have already moved to a new city, enrolled in new schools, visited a new church, and tried to meet new neighbors. Our old friends and family in Birmingham would've been hours away, and we would've been on an island in the moment of our greatest need.

But God was gentle. My mom turned the car around, and we stayed in Birmingham, close to friends, family, and a community that came around us. We remained close to doctors who knew my dad, other parents who knew how to care for my mom, and friends who knew how to have fun with us kids. Amid uncertainty and tragedy, the ability to laugh with friends was often the best medicine. Surrounded by our best friends, teammates, and classmates, I felt a level of comfort knowing that even when everything wasn't okay, we were still in good hands.

One week later and we would've been surrounded by strangers in a strange place. Yes, God could have and would have cared for us wherever we were, but he chose to keep us close to home, close to our people, and close to himself.

My dad's go-to verse during his treatment came from the prophet Isaiah: "Fear not, for I am with you; be not dismayed, for I am your God; I will strengthen you, I will help you, I will uphold you with my righteous right hand" (Isa. 41:10 ESV).

In the moment, it was often hard to experience God's strength or see his helping hand. But when I look back, I can see countless small graces in his timing. He was with us, most often through the love of friends and family close by. God gave us time at home with my dad, who couldn't work as the sickness progressed, time to see my dad read the Bible more than ever, and time to see the love between my mom and dad in a way we'd never seen before. In the years that followed, he gave us times of normalcy as a family: new traditions, happy memories, and the chance to laugh and talk about my dad once again.

The Shepherd Protects the Flock

Finally, God loved us through the church. No church is perfect, but God doesn't need perfection. After my dad passed away, we spent a few months looking for a new church. Our old church wasn't bad, but we needed one closer to our house, with a bigger network of support.

As a current seminary student, I would love to say that our most important criterion for choosing a church was finding a place that faithfully preached the Word and was committed to discipleship, evangelism, and missions. Or something like that.

But the reality was that we needed a place to be welcomed, and we found that in Brookwood (a place that, by the way, did all of the above). While we loved to worship at Brookwood, what drew us in was the way other parents—particularly those involved with the youth group—latched on to me and my brothers. We were new, we weren't super involved, but we were always remembered and welcomed and loved. Some people knew my dad, some didn't. But every Sunday, they were glad to see us.

But it wasn't only our one church, and it wasn't only other parents. Through other nearby churches and a local parachurch ministry, God provided a community of peers, older teenagers, and dads who became regular fixtures in our life. I mentioned earlier the impact that other dads had on my life, but older teenage guys were great too. Older high school guys who were leaders on retreats or at youth group Sunday morning were the same ones taking me home from football practice, babysitting when my mom was gone, or taking me out to eat before a big game. To my knowledge, no one told them to look out for us, but this desire was baked into their DNA as followers of Jesus. In the local church and the broader body of Christ, God gave my brothers and me a place to be at home.

More explicitly, however, God protected my family through the church. As my mom described, single parents are vulnerable in many ways, but a spiritual vulnerability accompanies the physical, financial, and relational uncertainties. Shortly after we'd joined our new church, my mom learned that some people wanted to follow us to our new church, but not for the right reasons. There was no physical threat, but emotionally and spiritually, it would have eroded the comfort and safety of our new church.

It was an awkward situation with a lot of backstory—but my mom needed a voice to stand up for her and fight in her corner. After she told our new pastor the situation, he promptly met with these people and told them to find a different church. He didn't doubt her or wait for something bad to happen; he went to bat for her. The shepherding duties of pastors and elders aren't solely expressed in gentleness, wisdom, and care in pastoral situations. Pastoring also means *defending* the flock. Our pastor protected our family, the people God had entrusted to him as an undershepherd of the Good Shepherd.

God's Persistent Grace

It's been over a decade since my dad passed away, and I think my experience wrestling with the grief and loss has looked a bit like a slow parabola over time. I didn't want to lose my dad or be different or receive special attention, and I was almost certainly a pill whenever someone tried to talk to me about my dad. Looking back, however, I can see touchpoints of God's grace along the way, and these almost always look like the persistence of friends and fathers who wouldn't leave us to grow up without them.

It would be impossible to give proper thanks to all the people who cared for us so lovingly over the past fourteen years. But thank you for playing the long game with us and for faithfully following Jesus into the messy lives of messed-up teenagers. There's no right way to reach the kids who grow up in single-parent homes, but your showing up, your curiosity, and your consistency made (and continue to make) all the difference.

Lastly, Mama, thank you. There are no words to capture your love in late nights and early mornings, the tears and lack of tears, the baseball games and debate tournaments, the missed curfews, the screaming matches, the acts of open warfare and silent acts of rebellion. You rock.

Sam, Ben, and I love you so much, and we're so grateful that God made you our mom. We all miss Dad, but I can't wait to share stories in heaven surrounded by friends one day.

Acknowledgments

I wrote my first book in the third grade, something about a lost puppy. I stapled lined notebook paper and turned it sideways, leaving space on every other page for my best friend Virginia to illustrate the story. It might have ended up in the trash can had not our third-grade teacher found our little creation lying around her classroom. Mrs. Scott arranged with the school librarian for us to read our book to all the kindergarteners and first graders during their story times (though Virginia reminds me that I was stingy with sharing the reading and not inclined to share her pictures either).

Ever since that first resounding success, my great dream has been to write books. I had the good fortune to learn at the start that no one puts a book into the world alone. Though writers begin in solitude, no one ever reads their words without a community that transforms words into manuscripts, converts manuscripts into books, and delivers books into readers' hands.

I've written in these pages about how becoming a single parent caused me to recognize my weakness. Writing a book forced me to confront my inadequacy all over again. Without the prayer and encouragement of so many people (certainly some I have neglected to mention here; please forgive me!), I could never have shared the story of my family's hardest challenge. But then I also would not have been able to share how faithful and loving God has been to us, and that would have been a great shame.

So I thank God for every one of you.

Virginia, you're still the best and truest friend anyone ever had, not to mention an artist who is never afraid to try something new and difficult. Where would I be without you? Not writing, that's for sure. Also, I'd laugh a whole lot less.

Three larger-than-life men knew exactly what I needed to get started. Collin Hansen gave me the vision to address the church alongside the single parent, saying that as an elder in his church, he needed to read the book too. Jim Barnette, perhaps the greatest encourager who ever lived, created opportunities everywhere he could for me to tell my family's story and cheered me on every day until he went to be with Jesus. And Cameron Cole was relentless, convinced that Jesus had given me what it took to write this book. His exuberant texts and high fives and cheers and absolute certainty gave me the strength to start the work and the perseverance to see it through. You're the best, Big C. RTR.

Cameron wisely suggested that I ask a team of folks to pray for me regularly. Deanna Barnette, Cora Causey, Hannah Dow, Katherine Galloway, Diane Griswold, Joelle Hamilton, Carolyn Lankford, Mary Little, Nancy Martin, Tracey Rector, and Tracy Yi: you are truly amazing women. I wish I could share all the ways each one of you encouraged me during this process, but that would require writing a whole other book. Knowing you were sharing in the work by praying very specifically for what I asked helped me not to feel alone. Each of you is a treasure, and I am so very grateful you're my sisters in Christ. Thank you for your faithfulness.

I was shameless in asking many other people to pray too, and I know you all did: Rebecca Ankar, Katey Blair, Jenny Burton, Garland Darden, Cindy Hodges, Caitie Morgan, Maggie O'Conner, Bragan Petrey, Christine Smith, Carla Ward, Leigh Whatley—you're my neighbors, but you kinda feel more like family. I also want to thank Cilie Cowin, Caroline Darby, Rachael Hellums, and Ashley McMahon for making sure I set aside time to laugh and relax along the way. And Gordon Bals, you've been such a kind, wise brother to me.

I work with the most ridiculously supportive people on the planet. Emily and Mary Beth, you both overflow with grace, love, and passion to make Jesus known. Your hearts are huge. Charlotte, I cannot thank you enough for taking the time to read every word and help me make it better. I wish I had one ounce of the creativity that gushes out of you every waking moment. Chelsea and Rebecca, I love that we get to learn, write, and edit together, but the real treasure is your warmth and friendship. Liz, you dragged me across the finish line, and I don't think this book would be here without you. Katherine, Jalyn, Laura, Anne, Danny, Sarah, Sandy, Kevin, Menendez, and my friends on the RPSC: you are an absolute treat. Only God could create a team that is *so much fun* to work with. Thank you for your prayers. I know you love me, and I love you too.

Lauren, thank you. Your wisdom and determination inspire me, not to mention your persistence in dragging me out to have fun when I didn't much want to. You and your amazing girls were in my heart the whole time I wrote this book.

To the single moms and dads who agreed to be interviewed: you made this book happen. I hope and pray that together we will spark conversations and stir hearts. You are not named, but you know who you are and so do I. Most important, God sees you. He sees your child. He knows what your family needs, and it is his delight to sustain you with steadfast love and drench you with his grace. Thank you for being willing to trust me with your stories. I know that was not easy.

Dale Williams, I feel like we are friends, even though we have not yet met. Your excitement about this project gave me much-needed boosts during the writing process, almost like you could sense when my courage was flagging. Kim Tanner, I learned a lot about editing from you, and the book is much better for the ways you continually pushed me to remember the entire audience. Emily Voss, the cover still makes me so happy—thank you for understanding what I was aiming for and making it look so warm and welcoming. The three of you care deeply for both the writer and her audience, and I am grateful for you.

To my brothers and sisters at Brookwood Baptist and Church of the Cross: I learned from you what the church can be to the lonely and hurting. Because God brought me to you, I have a vision of what it means that "we, though many, are one body in Christ, and individually members one of another" (Rom. 12:5 ESV). Within your "membership," that vision is lived reality. I want each single parent and single-parented child to experience what my family experienced in your warm embrace. Thank you for showing us Jesus.

Kathryn and Tom, Jane and Gene, you've embraced me as a sister and a daughter, even when I did not deserve it. (I guess that's what it means to be family, doesn't it?) Mom and Dad, you taught me so much, and I am grateful. Trip, you are the best brother I have ever had. And seriously, if you weren't my brother, you'd be one of my very best friends. You and Jenny have always, always had my back. I love you all.

To Tom, the gift I didn't see coming: I love you. I am still smiling.

And finally, to my boys. Good gravy, I love y'all so much. To Mac, who patiently talked me through many points of theology, read the manuscript, and then even agreed to write a chapter; to Sam, who came home and cooked dinner for me every night for two weeks so I could concentrate on writing; to Ben, whose complete confidence and affectionate reassurance fueled me in some of my most discouraged moments; I am in awe of you all. You show me so much love and grace. You fill my heart to bursting with gladness that God gave us to each other. I know your dad feels the same way.

Jesus, you are so very big and beautiful. You have done great things for us, and we are filled with joy.

Notes

Introduction: My Family's Story

1. C. S. Lewis, *A Grief Observed* (New York: HarperCollins, 1961), 1.

The State of Single-Parent Families and the Church Today

1. Paul Hemez and Chanell Washington, "Percentage and Number of Children Living with Two Parents Has Dropped Since 1968," United States Census Bureau, April 12, 2021, https://www.census.gov /library/stories/2021/04/number-of-children-living-only-with-their -mothers-has-doubled-in-past-50-years.html.
2. "Child Well-Being in Single-Parent Families," Annie E. Casey Foundation, August 1, 2022, https://www.aecf.org/blog/child-well -being-in-single-parent-families.
3. "Child Well-Being in Single-Parent Families."
4. "Single Mother Statistics," singlemotherguide.com, updated February 2, 2023, https://singlemotherguide.com/single-mother-statistics/.
5. University of Pennsylvania School of Medicine, "One-Parent Households Double Risk of Childhood Sexual Abuse," Science Daily, March 14, 2007, https://www.sciencedaily.com/releases/2007/03 /070313114303.htm.
6. "Marriage: Much More Than a Piece of Paper, Especially for the Kids," Institute for Family Studies, accessed January 26, 2023, https://ifstudies .org/ifs-admin/resources/education/ifs-marriage-fact-sheet.pdf.
7. Nicholas Zill, "How Family Transitions Affect Students' Achievement," Institute for Family Studies, October 29, 2015,

https://ifstudies.org/ifs-admin/resources/how-family-transitions
-affect-students-achievement-family-studiesfamily-studies-1.pdf.

8. Jean Twenge, "New Report: The Difference Family Structure Makes in Teens' Tech Use," Institute for Family Studies, October 31, 2022, https://ifstudies.org/blog/new-report-the-difference-family-structure -makes-in-teens-tech-use.

9. "Child Well-Being in Single-Parent Families."

10. Hemez and Washington, "Percentage and Number of Children Living with Two Parents."

11. Visit the National Fatherhood Initiative website, https://www.father hood.org/father-absence-statistic.

12. Blair Linne, *Finding My Father: How the Gospel Heals the Pain of Fatherlessness* (Charlotte, NC: The Good Book Company, 2021), 35.

13. Linne, *Finding My Father*, 35.

14. Stephen Kneale, "Raising Children Spiritually in a Single-Parent Context," Building Jerusalem, May 20, 2017, https://building jerusalem.blog/2017/05/20/raising-children-spiritually-in-a-single -parent-context/.

15. "Child Well-Being."

16. "Single Fathers: Neglected, Growing and Important," *Lancet* 3, no. 3 (March 2018), https://doi.org/10.1016/S2468-2667(18)30032-X.

17. Jim David and Michael Graham, "What Parents Should Know about the Great Dechurching with Jim Davis and Michael Graham," *The Rooted Parent* podcast, September 14, 2023, https://rootedministry .com/podcasts/rpdechurching/.

18. "48 Divorce Statistics in the U.S. Including Divorce Rate, Race, & Marriage Length," Divorce.com, updated January 3, 2023, https:// divorce.com/blog/divorce-statistics/.

19. Andrew Root, *The Children of Divorce, The Loss of Family as the Loss of Being* (Grand Rapids: Baker Academic, 2010), xx.

20. See Anna Harris, "Caring for the Single Moms in Your Church," Speak for the Unborn, April 19, 2021, https://speakfortheunborn .com/caring-for-the-single-moms-in-your-church/.

21. John Piper, "Is It Sinful to Be Pregnant before Marriage?" *Ask Pastor John* podcast, episode 976, Desiring God, December 14, 2016, https://www .desiringgod.org/interviews/is-it-sinful-to-be-pregnant-before-marriage.

22. Piper, "Pregnant." Piper is careful to note as well that if the woman was raped, she did not sin. But in these terrible cases, it is that much more imperative that the pregnancy and the child not be confused with the violent crime the baby's biological father committed. Nor should any woman feel compelled to explain that she became pregnant by rape, and yet when we ask questions designed to find out how the pregnancy happened, we only reopen the wounds of their trauma.

23. Piper, "Pregnant."

24. Kara Bettis, "Single Parent by Choice," *Christianity Today*, April 2021, 32.

25. Bettis, "Choice," 32.

26. Eric Tonjes, "Some Blunt Challenges to the Church about Single Parents," erictonjes.com, June 16, 2021, http://www.erictonjes.com /2021/06/some-blunt-challenges-to-church-about.html.

27. Tonjes, "Blunt Challenges."

28. Deut. 10:18; 14:28–29; 27:19; Jer. 22:3, among many places.

29. K. A. Ellis, "Loving the Widow," The Gospel Coalition, June 16, 2018, https://www.thegospelcoalition.org/conference_media/loving -the-widow/.

30. *Merriam-Webster*, s.v. "bereft," accessed August 8, 2023, https://www .merriam-webster.com/dictionary/bereft.

31. Ellis, "Loving the Widow."

32. Ellis, "Loving the Widow."

Chapter 1: God's Steadfast Love for the Single Parent and Their Child

1. The story is true; like all the testimonies here, her name and identifying details have been changed.

2. Ironically, Sarah banishes Hagar when she overhears her servant laughing. A simple laugh—no context—costs Hagar her livelihood and her home for her son. But Sarah herself not only laughs in the face of God's promise of a baby, she names her baby Isaac, which means "laughter." From her privileged position as Abraham's wife, Sarah enjoys security, whereas Hagar, as a single mother, is always one misstep away from disaster.

3. Ray Ortlund, "The Book of Job," The Gospel Coalition, March 4,

2014, https://www.thegospelcoalition.org/blogs/ray-ortlund/book
-of-job/.

4. Melissa LaCross, "How to Make Your Church an Encouraging
   Place for Single Moms," The Gospel Coalition, November 30, 2018,
   https://www.thegospelcoalition.org/article/church-encouraging
   -single-moms/.

5. John Greco, "Broken Vows, Broken World," The Gospel Coalition,
   November 17, 2017, https://www.thegospelcoalition.org/article
   /broken-vows-broken-world/.

6. Jen Wilkin, "You Have Heard That It Was Said" (lesson 5), *The
   Sermon on the Mount* (Nashville: Lifeway 2014). Wilkin has also
   written about the support her family felt from the local church. See
   Jen Wilkin, "The Church Is Not a Single-Parent Family," *Christianity
   Today*, November 23, 2016, https://www.christianitytoday.com/ct
   /2016/december/church-is-not-single-parent-family.html.

Chapter 2: God's Sufficiency in Our Not-Enoughness

1. Dale Ralph Davis, *1 Kings, The Wisdom and the Folly* (Geanies
   House, Fearn, Ross-shire, UK: Christian Focus, 2002), 214.

2. Davis, *1 Kings*, 208–9.

3. John Lin, "Raising the Widow's Son," Gospel in Life, July 15, 2015,
   https://gospelinlife.com/downloads/raising-the-widow-s-son-8975/.

4. Wendy Alsup, "Sister, God Sees You," The Gospel Coalition, October
   21, 2021, https://www.thegospelcoalition.org/article/god-sees/.

5. Alsup, "Sister, God Sees You."

Chapter 3: God's Courage in Our Fear

1. Mockingbird Ministries, *The Mockingbird Devotional: Good News for
   Today (and Every Day)* (Charlottesville, VA: Mockingbird Ministries,
   2013), 78.

2. C. S. Lewis, *The Problem of Pain* (New York: HarperOne, 2009), 27.

Chapter 4: God's Comfort in Our Grief

1. Clarissa Moll, *Beyond the Darkness: A Gentle Guide to Living with
   Grief and Thriving after Loss* (Carol Stream, IL: Tyndale Momentum,
   2022), 138.

2. Jaimie Troyal Shores, MD, Amputation, Johns Hopkins Medicine, accessed July 17, 2023, https://www.hopkinsmedicine.org/health/treatment-tests-and-therapies/amputation.

3. Barnabas Piper, "Barnabas Piper on the Pain of Divorce," interview by Christine Hoover, *Ministry Wives* podcast, North American Mission Board, September 29, 2020, https://www.namb.net/podcasts/ministry-wives-podcast/barnabas-piper-on-the-pain-of-divorce/.

4. Blair Linne, *Finding My Father: How the Gospel Heals the Pain of Fatherlessness* (Charlotte, NC: The Good Book Company, 2021), 48.

5. Linne, *Finding My Father*, 49.

6. Clarissa Moll, "Ask the Experts: Clarissa Moll on Caring for Grieving Teenagers," interview by Cameron Cole and Anna Meade Harris, *Rooted Parent* podcast, September 8, 2022, https://rootedministry.com/podcasts/ask-the-experts-clarissa-moll-on-caring-for-grieving-teenagers/.

7. John Henry Jowett, *The Silver Lining: Messages of Hope and Cheer* (New York: Revell, 1907), 123.

8. Moll, "Grieving Teenagers."

9. U2, "One," track 3 on *Achtung Baby* (Santa Monica, CA: Island, 1992).

Chapter 6: God's Presence in Our Loneliness

1. Because translation from one language to another is complicated, it's helpful to consult several translations when studying a particularly meaningful (or puzzling) verse. The Amplified Bible is a useful tool because it offers the regular Bible reader several options that a translator would be choosing from as they convert the text from Greek or Hebrew for English readers.

2. Charles Spurgeon, quoted in "Hebrews 13:5–7 Commentary," Precept Austin, updated November 30, 2022, https://www.preceptaustin.org/hebrews_135-7.

3. Brother Lawrence, *The Practice of the Presence of God* (New Kensington, PA: Whitaker House, 1982), 37.

4. Rosaria Butterfield, *The Gospel Comes with a House Key: Practicing Radically Ordinary Hospitality in Our Post-Christian World* (Wheaton, IL: Crossway, 2018), 31.

5. Butterfield, *House Key*, 111.

Chapter 8: God's Wisdom in Our Uncertainty

1. Tim Keller (@timkellernyc), "In the original language," Twitter, November 1, 2018, 6:23 a.m., https://twitter.com/timkellernyc/status/1057941067151171586?lang=en.
2. Kevin DeYoung, *Just Do Something: A Liberating Approach to Finding God's Will* (Chicago: Moody, 2009), 97.
3. Ray Ortlund, *Proverbs: Wisdom That Works* (Wheaton, IL: Crossway, 2014), 168.

Chapter 9: God's Grace in Our Shame

1. Curt Thompson, *The Soul of Shame: Retelling the Stories We Believe about Ourselves* (Downers Grove, IL: InterVarsity Press, 2015), 24. Throughout this chapter, the words of this refrain will be italicized, as they are in Thompson's book, to draw our attention to the lies shame tells.
2. Thompson, *Soul of Shame*, 24–25.
3. Brené Brown, "The Power of Vulnerability," TEDxHouston, December 2010, https://www.ted.com/talks/brene_brown_the_power_of_vulnerability/no-comments.
4. Thompson, *Soul of Shame*, 157.
5. So much so that the story of Peter's denial appears in all four gospel accounts. Clearly Peter was not ashamed of his failure; it seems likely he spoke of it often in the early church.
6. Just as with birthdays and Christmas, seek these kids out, especially if they are young, and help them make a card, buy a little gift, or plan a special surprise for their parent.

Chapter 10: Sin Separates Us, but the Gospel Makes Us Family

1. Vaneetha Rendall Risner, "No One Knows My Pain: How Pride Hides in Suffering," Desiring God, April 28, 2022, https://www.desiringgod.org/articles/no-one-knows-my-pain.
2. Kristin Bauslaugh, "Kristin Bauslaugh on Becoming a Widow and Single Parent," interview by Christine Hoover, *Ministry Wives* podcast, North American Mission Board, November 10, 2020, https://www.namb.net/podcasts/ministry-wives-podcast/kristin-bauslaugh-on-becoming-a-widow-and-single-parent/.

Afterword

1. Jonathan Tjarks, "Does My Son Know You? Fatherhood, Cancer, and What Matters Most," The Ringer, March 3, 2022, https://www .theringer.com/2022/3/3/22956353/fatherhood-cancer-jonathan -tjarks.